One Teenager at a Time

One Teenager at a Time

Developing Self-Awareness and Critical Thinking in Adolescents

Kari O'Driscoll

ROWMAN & LITTLEFIELD
Lanham • Boulder • New York • London

Published by Rowman & Littlefield
An imprint of The Rowman & Littlefield Publishing Group, Inc.
4501 Forbes Boulevard, Suite 200, Lanham, Maryland 20706
www.rowman.com

6 Tinworth Street, London SE11 5AL, United Kingdom

Copyright © 2019 Kari O'Driscoll

All rights reserved. No part of this book may be reproduced in any form or by any electronic or mechanical means, including information storage and retrieval systems, without written permission from the publisher, except by a reviewer who may quote passages in a review.

British Library Cataloguing in Publication Information Available

Library of Congress Cataloging-in-Publication Data Available

ISBN 9781475851458 (cloth)
ISBN 9781475851465 (paper)
ISBN 9781475851472 (electronic)

Contents

Preface	vii
Acknowledgments	ix
Introduction	1
1 First Lessons	5
Adolescent Brain Development 101	5
Learning and Communication Styles	7
2 Mindfulness	9
Educator Notes	9
Lessons	10
Energy Follows Intention	10
Anger Comes from Fear	13
Owning Our Stories	15
Mindfulness and Conflict	17
The Trap of Superlatives	19
Living Your Values	21
3 Compassion	23
Educator Notes	23
Lessons	23
Seeing Others in Pain	23
Differing Perspectives	25
Name-Calling v. Owning Your Emotions	27
Myths and Misperceptions about Bullying	29
What Don't You Know?	31
Self-Compassion	33
Alternative Forms of Wealth	35

4	Positive Mindset	39
	Educator Notes	39
	Lessons	39
	Altruism	39
	Deserving Joy	41
	Finding Joy	43
	Connection	45
	The Three Crowns	47
	Finding Meaning	49
5	Self-Worth	53
	Educator Notes	53
	Lessons	53
	Comparison as a Form of Self-Judgment	53
	Shame	55
	Fitting In	57
	Platonic Ideals	59
	Pressure to Perform	61
6	Stress, Anxiety, and Fear	63
	Educator Notes	63
	Lessons	64
	Going It Alone	64
	Fear, Wisdom, and Equanimity	66
	How We Freak Ourselves Out	68
	The Power of Story	70
	Rewiring the Brain to Chill	72
Appendix A: Activities		75
Mindfulness Worksheet		75
Compassion		81
Positive Mindset		86
Self-Worth		92
Stress, Anxiety, and Fear		97
Additional Activities		101
Appendix B: Skill Reference Guide to Lessons		107
About the Author		111

Preface

I began writing this series of discussion prompts and lessons when my daughters were in middle school. I spent years interacting with adolescents, chaperoning field trips, engaging in conversations, and learning about nonviolent communication and mindfulness. My interest in mental health and social development led me to seek out teachings by JoAnn Deak and Dan Siegel. I took classes from Mindful Schools and Brené Brown and The Chopra Center to expand my knowledge.

Research on educational best practices informed the structure of the lessons, and the content was developed over a period of four years. The more I learned about how our brains integrate and process information and the effect our thoughts have on our emotions and overall well-being, the clearer it became that the impact of mindfulness on the developing adolescent brain can be enormous.

Story is an incredibly powerful way to learn, which is why the lessons use story to introduce emotionally challenging concepts. Adolescents are incredibly socially driven; therefore, the group discussion format is a crucial element of this curriculum. Letting students lead discussions and engage in conversation allows them to frame abstract ideas just as their brains are able to appreciate non-concrete concepts.

The activities herein are designed to bring universal concepts to the individual level as well as adding practicality. Bringing the ideas home with guided meditation introduces mindfulness and engages different neural pathways.

These lessons address some of the most pressing issues facing adolescents—from ideas about their own worth, to dealing with stress and anxiety, to building community. With the exception of the first few exercises, there is no linear progression required. Educators are encouraged to "read the room" in their own student groups to determine which lessons will be the most vital on any given day so that they can engage with the students where they are in their own lives.

It will take a skilled facilitator to deliver this content since it offers students a great deal of ownership. They will learn to have difficult conversations without shutting down emotionally, derailing discourse by labeling or name-calling, and become more comfortable collaborating with those whose beliefs and biases are very different from their own. This will enable them to have complex interactions as adults without losing their own identity or feeling threatened.

Educators will need to have a clear eye toward behavior and rhetoric that is hurtful or potentially destructive and enforce strong classroom standards as well as refraining from adding their own ideas and opinions.

The lessons were also designed for maximum flexibility. Every school setting has its own challenges regarding time and resources, so a lesson can be delivered in one sitting or over a period of days during homeroom or advisory periods.

If you choose to break up a lesson into component parts, introduce the lesson during the first period and allow for some discussion. Revisit the discussion the next time you meet and ask if, upon reflection, other thoughts have surfaced. Add the activity during this second meeting. In a third meeting, take some time to debrief with students about discussion and activities and encourage them to share the impact it had on them in their daily lives since you last met. Close with the guided meditation.

Acknowledgments

No one is an island, especially when you're writing a book. I've used the work and brilliance of so many others to form my ideas and build upon as I created lessons, worked with students, and wrote meditations. Drs. Dan Siegel and Brené Brown have and continue to make amazing discoveries about the human brain and emotions and the interplay between the two. Dan Gottlieb and Kristin Neff and Christopher Germer have opened my eyes to the power of compassion and empathy, along with Pema Chödrön, Thích Nhất Hạnh, the Dalai Lama, bell hooks, and Maya Angelou and Gloria Steinem. There are countless others whose work I have devoured and appreciate greatly, but there isn't room here to list them all.

As for the people I know in real life, I first have to thank my daughters, Erin and Lauren, for teaching me what it is to be a mom, for trusting me with their thoughts and feelings and wisdom, and always supporting me on this writing journey of mine. To all their wonderful friends—Alex, SJ, Midori, Maia, Nia, Eleanor, Thomas, Sam, Moses—thanks for the amazing conversations and letting me bounce ideas off of you. I adore you all. Thereza, Jen L., Becky, Tracy, Jodie, Kathy, and Susan—your friendship and love and support buoy me when I need it most. Knowing you've got my back is immeasurably important.

Thanks so much to the amazing mentors I've had over the years who taught me that passion is one of the most important elements of any successful endeavor. Without that foundational belief, I might have given up on this project a long time ago.

To my fellow writers who have read bits and pieces of this and given me feedback to make it better, I am incredibly grateful. Tonya, Julie, and members of the Mindful Schools online community and the SEL for Washington community—your input has been so vital to this work. And to Bill in Arkansas and Seth and the students at Seattle's Recovery School, thank you for giving this curriculum a shot and helping me refine it.

Introduction

Every classroom has its own rules, and some portion of the first meeting should be spent talking about them with students. Here are two sets of overlapping rules you can copy, borrow, and adapt for your own purposes. The House Rules were adapted from The Rules of Cooperation from L'Arche Portland, a faith-based organization whose mission involves supporting individuals with intellectual disabilities. To reflect a positive mindset, they've been altered slightly.

1. **Abundance**—There is enough of what we all need if we cooperate.
2. **Equal Rights**—Your rights as a person are equal to mine, and we all have an equal responsibility to cooperate.
3. **Power Is Not a Tool Used Here**—Displays of physical power (hitting, slamming doors, etc.), threats, and passive-aggressive behavior (withdrawing, staying angry, refusing to talk, etc.) are not part of a cooperative environment. Anything that is designed to shut down conversation is counterproductive to our purposes.
4. **No Rescues**—If the thought of doing something for you makes me angry or resentful, I will not do it. If I think you're capable or simply avoiding it and I am compelled to "save" you, doing so will not further our work here.
5. **No Secrets**—Especially when I am feeling angry, afraid, or vulnerable, I will share my feelings knowing that I don't have to justify or defend them. This is a safe space for all of us.

The other set of guidelines was developed to ensure that there is ample space for everyone's voice and perspective.

RULES FOR DIFFICULT CONVERSATIONS

- Everyone at the table is here because they want to be (not because they are forced to be or have been guilted into it).
- Everyone has the same rights—we are all equals, and we all deserve to be heard and our perspectives respected.
- Even if we can't understand someone else's point of view or feelings, we respect their right to have them, and we all agree not to belittle anyone because of it.
- No name-calling.
- No ultimatums.
- No demands.
- No hate speech.
- We all agree to work our hardest to define a common goal and work toward it. Bringing up past resentments is not OK because it derails the conversation.
- No eye-rolling or turning away or other negative body language.
- If someone decides they can't be part of the conversation right now for any reason, they are allowed to leave, but they agree to be part of a future conversation designed to resolve any outstanding issues.
- Everyone agrees to own their part of the conversation and take responsibility for words or actions that might have caused others pain or frustration. There are multiple sides to every conflict. Nobody is ever all right or all wrong.
- Blaming and shaming, labeling others or ourselves, and using words like *always* and *never* will not move us forward and should be avoided.

CLASSROOM NORMS

It is not necessary for educators to have a personal mindfulness practice in order to do this work, nor does one have to be well versed in the basics of nonviolent communication. You should, however, be willing and able to curb your own opinion, place a higher value on student discussion than solutions or consensus, and be able to keep order without threats of punishment or using tactics such as shame or blame.

Sometimes, calling a student out in front of their peers seems unavoidable, but here are a few reasons why it's counterproductive:

1. *There are few things worse to an adolescent than being seen as inferior to their classmates.* During this time of increased social awareness, teens desperately want to be regarded positively by peers. Being part of a tribe is on par with basic survival to most adolescents, and when they are

shamed publicly, many find it incredibly difficult to recover from it. If a trusted adult is the one doing the shaming, the likelihood of a positive relationship surviving that is very low. This classroom needs to feel like a safe space, and it won't if the adult in charge is not trusted.
2. *Strong emotions interfere with our ability to hear and listen.* The higher our emotional intensity, the less we are able to process language accurately. When we are embarrassed, ashamed, or angry, the portions of our brain that are responsible for listening and learning are circumvented or muted.
3. *The more self-critical we are, the more self-absorbed we are.* While it's true that most teachers are motivated by helping students become better, if we fail to acknowledge a student's positive attributes, we are contributing to their isolation. Starting with a student's strengths and encouraging them to build on those things can help them become more internally motivated to improve. When someone points out what we've done wrong, we tend to focus on all of the other ways we don't measure up and, in turn, close down instead of forging alliances and finding support.
4. *Teens need adult-teen relationships they can trust.* To get the most out of their classes, teens and teachers need to cooperate and collaborate; however, if a teen doesn't trust their teacher or has formed a negative opinion of them, they will be more likely to give themselves permission to stop listening. Often, teachers sense this disdain and continue to push or call out these students, and this ultimately ends up making things worse.

Meeting teens where they are is incredibly important. Recognizing that they are highly susceptible to emotions—even if they don't show it—and planning our interactions with that in mind can make working with a struggling student much easier. Start with the positives, ask them where they could have used more support, and work together to make a plan. Approaching students with respect and setting aside our assumptions helps them get the most out of their education, and they need to be part of the process. The more they understand our wish for them to succeed, the more they will trust us.

FINAL NOTES ON THE CURRICULUM

Discussion

Ideally, every student will choose to engage in conversation with the group over time. Some students will be harder to draw out, and it's important that nobody feels forced to talk or be vulnerable. Because of each student's unique background, there may be some students in the class who struggle with some of the concepts. The goal isn't to have everyone agree or even talk enthusiastically—it is to have them practice engaging with peers around difficult topics.

Discussions can go above and beyond the time allotted, or they may be short and sweet—it depends entirely on the group and the students' interest and willingness to engage. Feel free to move along, ask students if they have ideas related to the topic that might extend conversations, or keep the discussion going for a subsequent meeting if students have a lot to say.

Activities

One effective way to keep students reflecting on the material between class periods is to give everyone a journal. This is also a great way to have those students who don't feel comfortable sharing in class explore the concepts on their own. There is no need to have students turn their journals in or show them to anyone.

There are a few activities throughout the curriculum that specifically ask students to journal about something, and if they decide they'd like to share their ideas with the class, they are more than welcome to do so.

Appendix A at the back of this book contains additional activities that can be used at any time.

Meditations

Students are invited to join the meditation but are not required to do so. Those who have suffered trauma may feel uncomfortable sitting in a room quietly with their eyes closed. There are recordings of the meditations accessible online should they want to try on their own at some point.

When reading the meditation to students, it is important to speak slowly and clearly and pause often to give students time to reflect and to practice sitting quietly and to quiet their minds. Each meditation should last approximately five minutes in total.

FINAL THOUGHTS

It is of the utmost importance that students understand that it's safe to engage in honest discussions around this material. There are no right or wrong answers, no judgment, and no winners or losers. The purpose of this curriculum is to give students opportunities to become emotionally savvy, develop self-awareness, and create strong relationships with themselves and their peers. It can take time for students to feel comfortable enough to open up, but if the facilitator is consistent in maintaining an open, compassionate dialogue among the participants, it will happen.

Chapter 1

First Lessons

ADOLESCENT BRAIN DEVELOPMENT 101

Knowledge is power, and knowing how their brains are developing can have an enormous impact on students' ability to understand their own motivations and emotions. It is vital that educators make and take the time to talk with students about the basics of adolescent brain development. There are several great resources online that offer visual aids for educators, but much of what is important for Social-Emotional Learning (SEL) purposes is summarized here.

Adolescence is a time of rapid growth, both with respect to physical maturation and brain development. This can cause challenges during middle and high school as kids begin to look more and more like little adults when their brains haven't quite caught up. It's tempting to expect tweens and teens to be more ready for complex decision-making than they actually are. Even if they seem proficient at some "adult" tasks, much of their most important brain growth has yet to happen.

The area of the brain called the prefrontal cortex (PFC) is responsible for reasoning ability, creative problem-solving, attention, and learning from mistakes. The PFC isn't fully developed until we are in our twenties, and even then, it can be hijacked by another portion of the brain called the amygdala—which is known as the emotion center. The amygdala is also known as the fight/flight/freeze center of the brain, and it serves a very important function, but it can make our lives difficult when the threats we face are more about who sits with us at lunch and less about being attacked by a hungry predator.

During the adolescent years (roughly between the ages of ten and twenty), the amygdala is physically larger than it ever will be again, which explains why teens can be emotionally volatile at times. Every piece of information

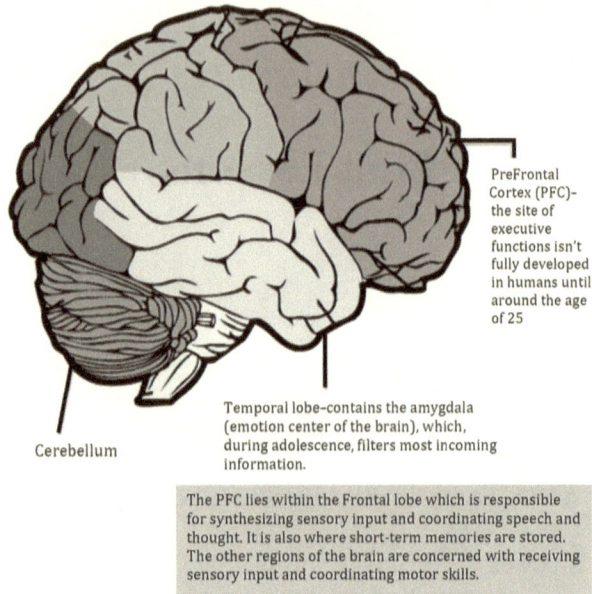

Figure 1.1 What Happens Where in the Brain. *Source*: Adapted from Massachusetts Institute of Technology, as featured in the *Wall Street Journal*.

that enters a teen brain is processed through this emotion center first, and if the trigger is big enough, it will shut down the brain's executive functions.

Figure 1.1 shows roughly how brain development occurs from left to right. Until the PFC is fully mature, our capacity to act more rationally and less emotionally is stunted. This is why it is important to be a little more patient with teens. Expecting an adolescent to "act like an adult" is similar to asking a child to swim the length of the pool at their first swim lesson. Executive functions need to be practiced for years before they can be relied upon, and the infrastructure needs to be there for us to access. The good news is that the more we practice, the better we get.

Key Point #1: The adolescent brain isn't fully ready for executive functions, but practice during these years is key to develop the "muscle" for rational thought and good decision-making. Learning to think critically, make abstract connections, and explore new ideas is important during the middle and high school years.

Acknowledging the power and physiology of the amygdala helps teens understand that it is normal to be ruled by their emotions during these years. Because this portion of the brain is responsible for fear, motivation, and physical responses to pain and pleasure, teens are more susceptible to anxiety, adrenaline, and addiction. Adolescents are more likely to make spur of the moment choices, process emotional slights as threats, and be less able to articulate their feelings without a lot of practice.

Key Point #2: We are biologically driven to feel overwhelmed with emotion between the ages of ten and twenty. Impulsivity and strong emotions are a key part of adolescence, and blaming or shaming won't change that. Learning from mistakes strengthens the PFC and helps ensure that as we get older, we will be less likely to act in ways that are counterproductive to our own health and well-being.

LEARNING AND COMMUNICATION STYLES

Before students embark on this important work, it is helpful for them to have an understanding of how they learn best. Someone who primarily processes information by listening (auditory) may struggle or push back when they're asked to read something and understand it. We tend to communicate with others instinctively in the way we prefer to learn—even if we don't realize it—so knowing how other people process information can help us communicate more effectively with them.

The VARK quiz is an online test that only takes a few minutes to complete and helps determine whether an individual's personal learning style is primarily visual, auditory, read/write, or kinesthetic. Students armed with this information can advocate more effectively for themselves by asking for what they need in any given situation. For educators, it can help to tailor your work by mixing up the way you present material so that it's meaningful for all of the students in the classroom.

Educators are highly encouraged to have their students take this quiz prior to diving into this curriculum. The quiz can be found here: http://vark-learn.com.

Chapter 2

Mindfulness

EDUCATOR NOTES

Jon Kabat-Zinn, a physician and world-renowned mindfulness educator, describes mindfulness as "the awareness that emerges through paying attention on purpose, in the present moment and non-judgmentally to the unfolding of experience moment by moment."[1] While that's comprehensive, it isn't necessarily something that resonates with adolescents. I prefer to talk about mindfulness as the ability to create mental space that allows us to slow down for a moment and assess.

The human brain is amazing and efficient and works to make connections, assumptions, and decisions almost before we are consciously aware of them. While that is sometimes really handy (such as when you're driving and a pedestrian darts out in front of you), it can be a little scary (such as when you eat half a pint of ice cream and can't really remember tasting it).

Mindfulness means that we are *not* multitasking, that we are making a conscious choice to align our physical actions with our thoughts, and that we are aware of how our emotions are driven by thoughts and vice versa. Learning to be open to what we smell, hear, say, feel, and taste instead of being miles away in our heads while we perform daily tasks is mindfulness. Understanding which of our subconscious beliefs and judgments is driving those actions and acting only after discerning the truth of those beliefs and judgments is mindfulness.

One way to get into the space of mindfulness is by asking questions. If you feel a particularly strong emotion for one reason or another, a knee-jerk response, stop and ask yourself, *What am I feeling right now?* Often, simply calling out the emotion is enough to open the door to that space where you can rest a beat and assess the situation. As emotions come to us, it is natural to unconsciously build stories to justify or explain them or rationalize our reactions. Mindfulness is about simply noting the feeling without labeling it as good or bad or acting on it right away.

If what you feel is uncomfortable or unpleasant (jealousy, anger, frustration), you can choose to ask, *Why am I feeling this way?* There may not be a ready answer, but it is a good reality check to at least ask. Because adolescents are so often at the mercy of their emotions, if they can begin to examine the stories that their emotions conjure up, they can gain new perspectives that will enable them to curb some of their strongest reactions.

Mindfulness relies on curiosity and acceptance, both of which lead to increased self-awareness and openness. When we are committed to practicing mindfulness, we are less likely to engage in negative self-talk that limits our belief in our own abilities.

In these lessons, students will begin to see mindfulness as a powerful tool to help them focus, relieve stress, and even bolster their immune systems.[2] They will understand how to use mindfulness to decrease aggression and negative stress levels, improve academic scores,[3] and help them feel more connected to their peers and family members.

Mindfulness isn't something anyone does continuously. Sometimes it feels good to daydream, and other times, to get everything done, we have to go on autopilot, and that's OK. However, in times of high emotion, when we feel overwhelmed, if we have trained our brains to slow things down and create space, we can keep from reacting automatically in a way that might cause harm to an important relationship or ourselves. The more we practice it, the easier it gets.

Before starting your first lesson on mindfulness, introduce the concept with this short video: https://www.youtube.com/watch?v=w6T02g5hnT4.

LESSONS

Energy Follows Intention

"You are no bigger than the things that annoy you."—Jerry Bundsen

Objective: Students will be introduced to the idea that the way they *think* about the world is directly related to the way they *interact with* the world. They will learn ways to redirect their thoughts and energies toward positive outcomes and possibilities instead of letting their brains do what they are prone to do, which is to worry and look for the negative things that could happen at any given time.

Tools:

- Discussion Prompt (5–10 minutes of introduction, 20+ minutes of discussion)
- Mind v. Body activity (10–20 minutes)
- Leaves Falling in a Stream meditation (5 minutes)

Discussion: Ask students to close their eyes for a minute and listen. Ask them not to think about ice cream, whatever they do. Describe an ice cream cone to them, even as you remind them they are not to think about ice cream. You might talk about the crisp, fresh waffle cone and the ice cream becoming shimmery at the edges as it begins to melt, threatening to run down the side of the cone. However you detail the image for them, let them know they are not to imagine ice cream while their eyes are closed.

When you're done, have the students open their eyes and talk to them about what it's like for our brain to NOT do something we tell it not to do. To not think about ice cream, our brain first has to identify what ice cream is, but by then, it's too late—we've already thought about ice cream. The trick of banishing an idea from our head is to replace it with something else instead, because our brain doesn't make much of the word *not* when it's paired with something else. Had you told them to think of spaghetti instead of ice cream, many of them would have been successful at not picturing ice cream.

This is a great illustration of how our energy and thoughts work. Energy has no agenda or goal, it just goes where it is pushed, placed, created, or sucked; therefore, when we spend our energy railing against or resisting or trying to deny something, we are actually *giving* that thing energy. Ask students to imagine a brick wall. Have them think about banging on it, kicking it, and pushing it. They're giving that wall their energy but not really getting anywhere. Their energy is simply bouncing off of that wall and making them more frustrated.

Now ask students to shift their attention to the sky above the wall. Ask them to focus on the thing that lies on the other side of the wall. Maybe by focusing on the thing they want that is on the other side they can think more creatively about how to get there. Can someone boost them up and over? Can they enlist others' help? Maybe they will get so caught up in the moment, looking for shapes in the clouds, that knocking down that wall or getting over it isn't nearly as important anymore.

When we choose to use our energy against something we don't want, it often feels bigger to us. We end up testing this thing, defining it, bouncing our energy off of it, and sometimes, that helps us decide how important it is to us to banish it. Often, turning our energy toward the thing we do want (like replacing the image of ice cream with spaghetti) becomes the way to a solution.

Key Point: When we focus on moving toward a goal, the parts of our brain that solve problems and think creatively are activated. When we focus on avoiding something, our fear centers are activated, and that shuts down the parts of our brain that think clearly.

Discussion Questions:

- Encourage students to talk about a time when they have focused on avoiding a particular outcome (i.e., not losing a lacrosse game) and what that felt like. Was it hard to focus? Were they panicked? What kind of self-talk was going on in their minds?
- Now have them talk about what it feels like to laser in on a *positive* outcome instead (i.e., winning that game). Does that feel different in any significant way in either their body or their mind? Does it affect the way they strategize or their self-talk?
- Have each student take a moment to quietly think of or write down at least one place in their life where they can make this shift right now.

Activity: Mind v. Body Worksheet (see Appendix A)

Meditation: Leaves Falling in a Stream

Read the following to students, pausing to let them remain still and quiet several times throughout. The entire meditation should last approximately five minutes.

Close your eyes and take two slow, deep breaths in and out through your nose.

Try to empty your brain of all thought and realize how hard it is to do. Even if you can manage it for a minute or two, it's normal for our brains to get sucked back in to reacting to something you hear or how your seat feels or worrying about an assignment or test you have tomorrow. It's pretty rare for anyone to be able to empty their head of all thought for very long, but this visualization can keep you from getting caught up in them for a few minutes and give your brain a rest.

Imagine you are sitting near a stream. Take a minute to picture the surroundings—maybe it's a shady forest or a sunny meadow. The stream can be wide or thin, deep or shallow, loud and gurgling or quiet. There is something large nearby that you can lean against—a rock or tree or bench. Sit for a minute and flesh out the scene.

Every time you have a thought, imagine it as a leaf falling from a nearby tree and slowly fluttering down to land in the water. As it comes into your line of sight—as you have the thought—notice it, watch it land, and see it float downstream from you. Don't chase it. Don't name it. Just notice it, and let it go.

There may be times when you have fifty thoughts in a minute and others when there are only a few, or one at a time. Let them all go. They are leaves in a stream. Sit for a minute and practice watching them go without describing them. Just notice.

When you're ready, take a very deep breath through your nose, and open your eyes.

Optional:

Ask students to reflect on the meditation and what it felt like, either to the group or in a journal. Let them know that this exercise changes their brain waves and effectively gives their brains a break from the constant work they do all day long—like resting during a physical workout.

Anger Comes from Fear

> "You may not control all the events that happen to you, but you can decide not to be reduced by them."—Maya Angelou

Objective: Students will learn to stop and analyze their anger before reacting. They will see that anger is a derivative emotion that stems from an overactive fear response and learn strategies to interrupt those reactions.

Tools:

- Discussion Prompt (5–10 minutes of introduction, 20+ minutes of discussion)
- Alternative Pathways activity (10–20 minutes)
- Take Your Emotional Temperature meditation (5 minutes)

Discussion: Ask students to think about the last time they were really angry. Have them try to analyze what it was that made them so upset and take a minute to see if they can get to the root cause. It can be helpful to ask a series of "why" questions to continue digging deeper and deeper.

One way to illustrate this is to have students imagine letting a pet dog outside for a moment. The dog races off after a squirrel out into the street and nearly gets hit by a car. Most people would chase after the dog, screaming, and many would be angry with the dog and want to punish it for that behavior, or we would direct anger at the driver of the car. When we really think about this situation, we realize our anger stems from a fear of the dog getting hurt, and the desire to punish the dog comes from wanting to prevent them from ever doing such a thing again.

Ask students to reflect on whether other "unpleasant" emotions also come from fear. When we are judgmental of someone is it because we are afraid? Is being afraid in this way either because we feel we aren't as good as they are or because we are a lot like them and we wish we weren't? Often, when we see something bad happen to someone else, our brains try to make us feel better and safer by making a list of all the reasons that could never happen to us (because we are better/smarter/luckier than that person).

Discussion Questions:

- Ask students if they can trace a strong feeling of rage or anger back to a specific fear. Is anyone willing to share an example?
- Have students talk about examples in the news or their own community or families where a disagreement erupted because of someone's fear. Can they brainstorm ways that the situation could have been different if the fears were addressed without anger?
- Ask whether there are other difficult emotions that students think are related to fear.

Activity: Alternative Pathways (see Appendix A)

Meditation: Take Your Emotional Temperature

Read the following to students, pausing to let them remain still and quiet several times throughout. The entire meditation should last approximately five minutes.

Close your eyes and take a deep breath. Let it out through your mouth. Think about the primary emotion you're feeling right now. It might be hard to separate some of them out, and if it is, it's OK to just note all of the emotions you're feeling right now:

<blockquote>bored anxious worried restless sad peaceful happy
angry frustrated</blockquote>

Can you see the words in your mind, floating against a black background, shifting and changing? Is there one that stands out more than the others? Try not to get caught up in the story behind the emotions or explain why or try to figure it out. Just note what you're feeling more than anything else. If there is one word that stands out more than another, focus on it, and see if you can feel where that affects your body. If you're angry or frustrated, maybe it shows up as tightness in your chest. If you're happy, maybe there's a warm glow in your belly. Don't think about why you feel the way you do or judge whether it's good or bad; just notice it.

Why does your emotional temperature matter? Because our brains work so quickly to react to situations we are in that, depending on the temperature, we will say and do different things.

Think about how slowly things move when it's cold. Imagine your thoughts and words like honey. When your emotional temperature is cool (peaceful, joyful, happy, etc.), you are more likely to react to a new or unexpected situation with curiosity and optimism. You are less likely to jump to conclusions.

When it's warm, honey runs quickly. If you are feeling anxious or fearful, angry or frustrated, you are more likely to assume bad intent or negative outcomes. Your reactions are swift and decisive.

Think about a time when someone said or did something to you and you reacted out of anger or fear. Can you think of another time when you were feeling happy and peaceful and a similar incident occurred except this time you were calm and able to handle it?

When you're ready, take a deep breath and open your eyes. Write down the top two or three emotions you're feeling at this moment. That is your emotional temperature. At any given time, you are feeling a collection of different things, but there are always one or two that are more prevalent than the others. You can take your emotional temperature anytime you want to by just taking a moment to breathe and tune in to what you're feeling.

Owning Our Stories

"Don't be satisfied with stories, how things have gone with others. Unfold your own myth."—Rumi

Objective: Students will be taught to recognize that their brain is always making up stories in order to make sense of the world. Often, we react emotionally to certain situations, and our minds race to keep up by filling in the gaps in our knowledge so that we can try to understand why we feel a certain way. They will learn that stopping to ask themselves what they don't know (what their brain is assuming) is a powerful way to remain calm and relaxed in a situation that is frustrating.

Tools:

- Discussion Prompt (5–10 minutes of introduction, 20+ minutes of discussion)
- Dream Analysis activity (10 minutes)
- Basic Mindfulness meditation (5 minutes)

Discussion: Tell the students the story of a mother who headed into the bathroom and didn't notice that the toilet paper was all gone until it was too late. As she sat there, fuming, she remembered all the times she had reminded her children to replace the toilet roll when they were the one to finish it.

The mother stormed out of the bathroom intending to round up her kids and lecture them about being disrespectful and never listening to her and found her youngest child mopping up a puddle of iced tea from the kitchen floor. The startled child looked up to see his parent holding an empty cardboard tube in her hand and apologized instantly—saying he had left the bathroom in search of another roll of toilet paper but tripped and spilled his drink and got distracted as he cleaned up the mess on the floor.

The mother's anger instantly deflated, and she felt awful as she realized that the story she had made up in her mind about her lazy, disrespectful children was completely untrue. The only "truth" was that there was no toilet paper in the bathroom. The rest of the backstory was completely fabricated in her mind.

Discussion Questions:

- Ask the students to think about a time when they made assumptions about someone else and accused them of something based on those assumptions. Can they see how we often tell ourselves stories about why other people do things and put ourselves in the role of "good guy"?
- Are there times they can think of when they were accused of doing something they didn't do or that they had a perfectly good reason for doing something? What was their reaction? Did they get defensive and angry?
- Ask that the next time they find themselves getting angry with someone, they take a moment to remember this discussion. Can they ask themselves whether there might be information they don't have?

Activity: Dream Analysis (see Appendix A)

Meditation: Basic Mindfulness Meditation

Read the following to the students, pausing to let them remain still and quiet several times throughout. There is much less instruction in this meditation, so students should be given ample opportunity to sit quietly and practice coming back to their breath. The entire meditation should last approximately five minutes.

Find a comfortable position to sit in and close your eyes. Take a few deep breaths to clear your mind and settle in. As you relax, choose one thing to focus on—it can be the in-and-out cycles of your breath, a particular word, or a picture of something in your mind. Notice how that focal point feels—warm or cool, soft or supportive, centering, peaceful. Here is where it gets hard not to let your brain take over and create a story about why or who.

If your mind does start to wander, just gently bring it back to that one focal point. Repeat the word in your mind or count your breaths. No stories. No judgment. No getting upset with yourself for how often your mind wanders.

Sit like this quietly for a minute, bringing your mind back to your focus as many times as you need to. Pretend that you are outside your mind, just watching how it works and noticing its tendencies. Maybe today it is fairly quiet and compliant, or perhaps it really wants to distract you. Just notice, and bring it back.

When you're ready, take an extra deep breath, and open your eyes.

Mindfulness and Conflict

"No man can think clearly when his fists are clenched."—George Jean Nathan

Objective: Students will learn about the effects of strong emotions on constructive discourse. They will examine ideas of conflict and power.

Tools:

- Discussion Prompt (5–10 minutes of introduction, 20+ minutes of discussion)
- Knot Journaling activity (10 minutes)
- Different Perspectives meditation (5 minutes)

Discussion: Functional MRI (magnetic resonance imaging) is a tool researchers and physicians often use to look at the brain while we are awake and going through our normal activities. It is possible to determine which portions of the brain are most active or inactive during certain tasks or emotional states, and these studies have shown that the more intense our emotions are, the less we are able to listen effectively. That means that the more upset we are about something, the less likely we are to really hear what someone else is saying. We might think we understand what they are saying, but the portion of our brain dedicated to processing auditory information is hampered by our brain's emotional centers.

This is important information when we think about what happens when we are in conflict with someone. It is also important to note that it is possible to disagree with someone without being in conflict with them—think about conversations you might have with a friend or family member about music or the kind of food you prefer. Generally, disagreement doesn't involve a strong emotional response, but conflict does. That is because conflict is about power.

We are either in conflict with someone because we are actively trying to influence them in one way or another (i.e., we feel as though we have power), or we are defensive because we are feeling as though they have power over us and we are trying to shift the balance. When a power struggle starts, often the issue or the goal takes a back seat to the desire to win, and because the listening centers of our brain are not working properly when we are emotionally triggered, it is difficult to think about how to find a mutually agreeable solution.

Discussion Questions:

- Have students discuss their perspectives on the difference between disagreement and conflict. Do they feel different, sound different, and/or look different?
- Can students identify how disagreement turns into conflict and provide examples? Is it possible to move back from conflict to disagreement?
- Ask students to talk about the kinds of conflict they encounter most in their lives and whether they can imagine ways to dial down the emotion so as to get to a place where they can hear what the other person is saying. What are the overriding emotions they feel when they're in conflict with another person? Does it depend on the person?

Activity: Knot Journaling (see Appendix A)

Meditation: Different Perspectives

Read the following to students, pausing to let them remain still and quiet several times throughout. Students should be given ample opportunity to sit quietly during the meditation and sketch the scene in their mind. The entire meditation should last approximately five minutes.

Find a comfortable seat and close your eyes. Take a few deep breaths in and out to clear your mind of any random thoughts.

Imagine you are inside a cabin surrounded by trees. You are lying on the floor in front of the fireplace when you hear the sound of rushing water. You think it must be raining, but it doesn't matter. You are warm and comfortable, and the roof is strong.

Now, imagine that, instead of lying on the floor, you have moved to a comfortable chair in the corner. Maybe you're reading a book or just daydreaming. You still hear the sound of rushing water, and you look out the window to see only blue sky. Your idea of what is happening is much different at this point. You know the sound is not rain. However, you still aren't worried because there is no water visible inside the cabin, so you know you're safe. Maybe you decide that there is someone outside using a hose.

Finally, imagine standing in the doorway to the cabin, looking out at the beautiful forest, when you hear the sound of rushing water. You can see that it isn't rain nor is someone using a hose, and if you take a step out onto the deck, you realize that what you're hearing is actually the sound of cars driving past on the wet road just up the way.

Sit for a moment, and let yourself move from the floor to the chair to the doorway and acknowledge how your perspective changes as you move. Think about how this is true for all of us in a relationship; that we each have a unique way of looking at the world, and that uniqueness determines how we interact with each other. Often, when we are in conflict, we fail to recognize our own limitations in viewpoint and think that our way of seeing things is the only way to see them.

When you're ready, take a deep breath, and open your eyes.

The Trap of Superlatives

> "I've learned that people will forget what you said, people will forget what you did, but people will never forget how you made them feel."—Maya Angelou

Objective: Students will learn to pay attention to the words they use to express strong emotions. They will think about why we exaggerate and how it can make unpleasant situations feel worse than they are.

Tools:

- Discussion Prompt (5–10 minutes of introduction, 20+ minutes of discussion)
- Superlatives Journaling activity (10 minutes)
- Basic Mindfulness meditation (5 minutes)

Discussion: Don Miguel Ruiz is the author of the book *The Four Agreements*, which can help us understand the things we do out of habit that can make life more difficult. *The Four Agreements* gives us a framework for breaking those habits and building stronger relationships with ourselves and others. The first agreement is, "Be impeccable with your word. Say only what you mean."

The use of words like *always, never, nobody,* and *everyone* is common in everyday language (these words are known as superlatives), but when we stop to think about the way they are used, it is important to note that they are very rarely accurate. When we complain, "Nobody ever lets me choose" or "Everyone hates me," it may seem harmless and obvious that we don't really mean every single time, but using words in this way sends a signal to the emotion centers in our brain that a situation we find ourselves in is permanent and we are powerless to change it.

Nelson Mandela famously said, upon his release from prison, "It is not my custom to use words lightly. If twenty-seven years in prison have done anything to us, it was to use the silence of solitude to make us understand how precious words are, and how real speech is in its impact on the way people live and die."[4] Public personalities use superlatives as a tactic to spur people to action, such as how Hitler convinced his followers that *all* Jewish people were evil. These kinds of words reduce complicated issues to either/or, all-or-nothing scenarios, and obscure the nuances and mitigating circumstances that are really present and help us to find common ground.

Discussion Questions:

- Have students explore reasons why they might use words like *never/always* or *nobody/everyone*. Does it have to do with strong emotions? Are the words helpful when trying to convince someone else to do something (or not do something)? Is it simply a habit?
- Students can also talk about how they respond to people who tend to exaggerate things. Is it harmless, or does it have the effect of making it harder to take them seriously?
- How powerful are words? Are there times when we think they aren't powerful at all? Can students cite examples of both in their own lives?

Activity: Superlatives Journaling (see Appendix A)

Meditation: Basic Mindfulness meditation

Read the following to students, pausing to let them remain still and quiet several times throughout. There is much less instruction in this meditation, so students should be given ample opportunity to sit quietly and practice coming back to their breath. The entire meditation should last approximately five minutes.

Find a comfortable position to sit in and close your eyes. Take a few deep breaths to clear your mind and settle in. As you relax, choose one thing to focus on—it can be the in-and-out cycles of your breath, a particular word, or a picture of something in your mind. Notice how that focal point feels—warm or cool, soft or supportive, centering, peaceful. Here is where it gets hard not to let your brain take over and create a story about why or who.

If your mind does start to wander, just gently bring it back to that one focal point. Repeat the word in your mind or count your breaths. No stories. No judgment. No getting upset with yourself for how often your mind wanders.

Sit quietly for a minute in this state, bringing your mind back to your focus as many times as you need to. Pretend that you are outside your mind, just watching how it works and noticing its tendencies. Maybe today it is fairly quiet and compliant or perhaps it is really wanting to distract you. Just notice and bring it back.

When you're ready, take an extra deep breath, and open your eyes.

Living Your Values

> "When your values are clear to you, making decisions becomes easier."—Roy Disney

Objective: Students will be prompted to think about how their everyday choices reflect their values (or not) and how to be more intentional about living in alignment with the beliefs that are most important to them.

Tools:

- Discussion Prompt (5–10 minutes of introduction, 20+ minutes of discussion)
- Personal Crest activity (10 minutes)
- Walking the Path meditation (5 minutes)

Discussion: Tell the students the story of a teacher who asked her classroom of middle school students to show him or her their Instagram posts for the last six months. They were all assured that the content would remain confidential and that it would not be used to punish or stigmatize anyone.

As the teacher went through each account and made notes, the students were asked to jot down a few words that indicated what they wanted to be known for—sports ability, dedication to academics, being the "funny one," and so on. The teacher met with each individual student to compare notes, and in nearly every case, the student was surprised to hear what the teacher believed was most important to them, given their social media posts.

One girl, upon hearing that the teacher identified her most deeply held values as her physical appearance and having fun, told the teacher that she was a straight-A student who aspired to be a cancer researcher. Another student said that her most deeply held values involved family, despite the fact that all of her Instagram posts featured her by herself.

Discussion Questions:

- Ask students to think about whether their own personal values are well defined or not. Have they changed over time? Who informs their values?
- Have students discuss whether or not it's important to engage in actions that reflect their individual values throughout the day. Is it possible to tell if someone isn't living their values? Does it change how we feel about people if we hear them saying they believe in one thing and their actions show differently?

- What happens when we call others on their actions or language not matching up with their stated values?

Activity: Personal Crest (see Appendix A)

Meditation: Walking the Path

As you talk students through this meditation, be sure to pause often and allow for many quiet opportunities for them to practice coming back to the breath. This entire mindful moment should last anywhere from five to ten minutes.

Find a comfortable position, and softly close your eyes. Take a deep breath to clear any stray thoughts from your mind.

Imagine that you are entering a brightly lit building and, once inside, you see several paths stretching out in front of you. There is no rush to choose one, so you can stand and observe as long as you want to. Overhead, there are signs pointing to different areas where you can dance and sing, where you can choose to spend time quietly reading, where you can join loved ones, or pursue activities that are important to you, such as sports or gaming or art.

As you begin to move down one path, signs from the paths you didn't choose flash in front of you from time to time and side routes open up as possibilities. You can decide whether to shift your path or not at any time. If you feel you've chosen a path that isn't really fitting anymore, create a new one in your imagination to step onto. Name it. Notice what it feels like and what you think about as you step onto it. Take a minute to think about how you decide which path is the right one for right now.

Stop for a minute, and see if you can decide what one of your most deeply held values is. Is it family or hard work? Creativity or social justice? Rest or laughter? When you have one key value in your head, imagine a path opening up before you that nurtures that value and lets you move forward.

See all of the other signs fall away as you take a few steps forward, and think about what it feels like to be on this path that represents your true self and something that is incredibly important to you. Sit with that feeling for a minute before taking another deep breath and opening your eyes.

NOTES

1. Kabat-Zinn, Jon. January 2017. "Me Me Me." Video retrieved from https://www.mindful.org/jon-kabat-zinn-defining-mindfulness/.

2. https://www.ncbi.nlm.nih.gov/pmc/articles/PMC4940234/.

3. https://www.ncbi.nlm.nih.gov/pmc/articles/PMC5405439/.

4. Mandela, Nelson. February 11, 1990. "On Release from Prison." Cape Town, South Africa.

Chapter 3

Compassion

EDUCATOR NOTES

Compassion is essential for living in a community. Being able to empathize with others and willing to proactively work to make things better are important components of strong, healthy relationships. Because human beings are inherently social, we need to be able to relate to others to thrive, and compassion drives us to feel a connection with something larger than ourselves. When we feel this connection, we are spurred to make positive changes in our communities that ultimately benefit everyone. It is often more compelling to help others than it is to help ourselves, but in reacting to others' needs, we are truly helping ourselves as well.

Living in a society that praises individualism and individual accomplishments can often feel at odds with compassion, so exploring ideas of empathy and compassion during adolescence can help build that "muscle" that enables us to reach out to others even as we are pressured to perform.

LESSONS

Seeing Others in Pain

"Empathy is about finding echoes of another in yourself."—Mohsin Hamid

Objective: Students will examine their individual reactions to seeing others in emotional pain and think about whether there are limits to their willingness to be compassionate.

Tools:

- Discussion Prompt (5–10 minutes of introduction, 20+ minutes of discussion)
- Struggling with Compassion activity (10 minutes)
- Lovingkindness meditation (5 minutes)

Discussion: Often, when we see someone else in emotional pain, we do one of two things; turn away or reach out to them. When we make the choice to reach out to them, it is often in spite of our own discomfort with their pain, and that in and of itself is an act of courage. At that point, we have three choices: we can try to fix things for or with them, we can get down in the pit of sadness with them and hang out, or we can try something called "holding space."

Holding space is simply about acknowledging someone else's despair and sadness without offering advice, trying to change their perspective or diminish their feelings, actively taking on their emotions as our own, or trying to fix anything. It is a way to recognize and accept someone else's right to feel whatever they are feeling and allow them to process those strong emotions without judgment. It has the effect of letting the other person know they aren't alone and can be quite powerful.

Discussion Questions:

- Talk about which of the three strategies students generally choose when they see someone else hurting: empathizing deeply (getting in the pit with them), fixing/making it better (this can include attempting to talk them out of feeling the way they feel), or holding space.
- Is there one reaction that feels more caring? Is there one that feels more effective? Can they find examples of each of the three in their own lives?
- Ask students to think about what happens when they are struggling. Do they seek out people who will suffer with them, who will try to fix things or change the situation, or those who are simply loving and supportive? Are there times when one of these feels better than another? Why?

Activity: Struggling with Compassion (see Appendix A)

Meditation: Lovingkindness

Educators can introduce this meditation to students by explaining that it is a fairly basic compassion meditation, often called "metta" or "lovingkindness." The goal of these meditations is to first focus on finding compassion for yourself and then extending it outward to encompass kindness and love for all beings. As always, be sure to allow for ample quiet time as students breathe and practice sitting quietly.

Begin by finding a comfortable position and closing your eyes. Take a few deep breaths in and out to settle into this place and clear your mind of other thoughts that might linger.

Once you feel relaxed and your mind is free from thoughts, imagine that each breath you take in fills you with warmth and light. Each breath is designed to feed you, to nourish you, to keep you going. After a few rounds of this breath, focus on feeling gentle and kind toward yourself, accepting yourself for who you are. Keep breathing.

After several more rounds of breaths focusing on kindness, continue to breathe deeply, and say to yourself, "May I be safe. May I be healthy. May I be happy."

Repeat these phrases slowly a few times until you begin to feel that self-love within you in the form of warmth and light.

Now, imagine that as you exhale, you are extending some of that warmth and light outward to others without diminishing it inside yourself. It is simply amplifying, and you are the source. Much like using your candle's flame to light another candle, it doesn't extinguish your flame to share it.

As you breathe, continue stoking your warmth and light as you inhale, and as you exhale, think to yourself, "May all beings be safe. May all beings be healthy. May all beings be happy." Take several more rounds of breath as you repeat these phrases and send warmth and light out to all beings.

When you are ready, take an especially deep breath in, and slowly open your eyes.

Differing Perspectives

> "Empathy is the most mysterious transaction that the human soul can have, and it's accessible to all of us, but we have to give ourselves the opportunity to identify, to plunge ourselves in a story where we see the world from the bottom up or through another's eyes or heart."—Sue Monk Kidd

Objective: Students will explore the idea that the way they see the world is just one of many different ways to see it. They will be given the opportunity to view things in a completely different way and explore how doing so might lead to more compassionate relationships with people whose beliefs are not the same as theirs.

Tools:

- Discussion Prompt (5–10 minutes of introduction, 20+ minutes of discussion)
- Assigning Feelings activity (10 minutes)
- Changing Suffering to Caring meditation (5 minutes)

Discussion: Educators can use the following two stories to introduce the concept of how different people can see the same thing in very unique ways.

During a TED Talk, Derek Sivers first talks about the difference between how addresses are noted in Japan and the United States. He asks the audience to imagine a traveler from Japan asking an American for the name of the block they're on. The person is confused, and responds, "The blocks don't have names. The streets have names. The blocks are simply the empty spaces between streets." He then goes on to illustrate how the exact opposite is true in Japan—the blocks are named, but the streets are not—they are simply the empty spaces between blocks.[1]

The second story is about some rural villages in China. In these places, the local medical professional is paid by the townspeople every single day. He or she comes by each house in the morning to collect coins from a box placed outside for that purpose. If he or she happens upon a house where there is no money in the box, that is a message that there is someone inside who is sick and needs care. In these villages, the physician is only paid when the people in his or her care are healthy. They believe that this is the best way to ensure that the physician is doing all they can to prevent everyone from getting sick in the first place.

These two stories illustrate the idea that two seemingly opposite things can exist and that both can work.

Discussion Questions:

- Without judging whether one is right and another wrong, engage students in conversation about perspectives. What effect did these stories have on them?
- Ask students to talk about how often they judge others based on their own idea of what is "normal." Can they imagine that these ideas might seem odd in a different context or culture?
- Can anyone provide an example of a story like this where they were surprised to learn of a very different way of being in the world? Has anyone had to explain to someone else how their perspective is vastly different? How did they handle that? What did they learn from it?

Activity: Assigning Feelings (see Appendix A)

Meditation: Changing Suffering to Caring

As always, make sure you are allowing plenty of opportunities for students to sit quietly and breathe and practice keeping their minds focused and still.

In any given moment, there is a lot of suffering in the world that we are almost constantly reminded of by the media and our loved ones. It is easy to feel overwhelmed by events that are out of our control, and this meditation is a great way to extend compassion for those who are struggling even when we are powerless to change it.

Find a comfortable position, and close your eyes. Take several deep breaths as you settle in, and clear your mind of all thoughts. Once you are ready, I want you to imagine that the state of suffering has a color associated with it. As you breathe in, see that color as a kind of smoke that you inhale. It can't hurt you, and it won't stay inside because it isn't yours. It doesn't belong to you. You are simply the agent of change for this struggle.

By the magic of meditation and compassion and imagination, as the suffering breath reaches your lungs, it is converted into love. You can tell because the color changes. Imagine the color of love, and see it replace the color of pain in your lungs.

Exhale, and imagine that you have replaced a little bit of the suffering in the world with a brighter, cleaner love. Continue to breathe in the suffering and breathe out love. You can't change it all, but you're making a difference.

Breathe this way for a few minutes. When you're ready, inhale one clear, clean breath and exhale one clear, clean breath to reset, and open your eyes.

Name-Calling v. Owning Your Emotions

> "Compassion will cure more sins than condemnation."—Henry Ward Beecher

Objective: Students will talk about how often we resort to labels when there is a conflict to distance or protect ourselves. They will discuss the emotions behind conflict and determine whether they can act in more compassionate ways when they disagree with others.

Tools:

- Discussion Prompt (5–10 minutes of introduction, 20+ minutes of discussion)
- Accepting Circle and Emotional Mirror activities (20 minutes)
- Lovingkindness meditation (5 minutes)

Discussion: Often, when we are hurt or bothered by someone else's words or behavior, we dismiss them with a label: "liar," "jerk," "idiot," "slut," and so on. In fact, this habit is so well ingrained for most of us by the time we are in our teens, we do it without even stopping to acknowledge that what is lying beneath our anger or frustration is fear or hurt feelings. We simply jump to labeling the person we are angry with and use that label to justify our actions and attitudes toward them. This is a distancing tactic that divides us and shuts down conversations instead of bringing us together in the community. Because of that, it is ultimately harmful to everyone involved.

One problem with name-calling is that it defines someone else, even if that definition is only temporary. When someone lies—which, let's face it, we all do from time to time—we often call them a liar. That puts the other person into a pretty tight box and has the effect of defining them by their biggest mistake or worst act, and it tends to make people defensive.

If, instead, we are able to take a breath and say, "Wow, I'm really upset that you didn't tell me the truth," they have a little more wiggle room. They might still get defensive, but being called out for one act leaves the opportunity for forgiveness and compromise open. Labeling someone a liar sends the message that they are forever in your mind a horrible person, and it says that you aren't interested in working things out because you've already decided that they aren't going to change.

Expressing how you feel might still lead to the other person getting defensive, but at least they know how their actions have affected you, which is really the point, right? It seems obvious that getting upset and calling someone a name means that you're upset and your feelings are hurt, but think about the difference between "You suck!" and "Man, it really bothers me that you did that."

Discussion Questions:

- Have students talk about how they might react differently to name-calling than they would to someone telling them how they feel. How might it shift the dynamic of the conversation?
- Ask students to talk about what it would be like to be the person who refrains from name-calling and, instead, expresses their feelings. Does that feel too vulnerable? Does that take more courage than striking out in anger? What is the hardest part of that?
- Have students imagine that the next time someone labels them, instead of getting angry and defensive, they simply ask what the other person is feeling. Ask them to imagine what it would be like to encourage the other person to talk about what is upsetting them and how they might react if someone did that for them.

Activities: Accepting Circle and Emotional Mirror (see Appendix A)

Meditation: Lovingkindness

Educators can introduce this meditation to students by explaining that it is a fairly basic compassion meditation, often called "metta" or "lovingkindness." The goal of these meditations is to first focus on finding compassion for yourself and then extending it outward to encompass kindness and love for all beings. As always, be sure to allow for ample quiet time as students breathe and practice sitting quietly.

Begin by finding a comfortable position and closing your eyes. Take a few deep breaths in and out to settle into this place and clear your mind of other thoughts that might linger.

Once you feel relaxed and your mind is free from thoughts, imagine that each breath you take in fills you with warmth and light. Each breath is designed to feed you, to nourish you, to keep you going. After a few rounds of this breathing, focus on feeling gentle and kind toward yourself and accepting yourself for who you are. Keep breathing.

After several more rounds of breathing focused on kindness, continue to breathe deeply and say to yourself, "May I be safe. May I be healthy. May I be happy."

Repeat these phrases slowly a few times until you begin to feel that self-love within you in the form of warmth and light.

Now, imagine that as you exhale, you are extending some of that warmth and light outward to others without diminishing it inside yourself. It is simply amplifying, and you are the source. Much like using your candle's flame to light another candle, it doesn't extinguish your flame to share it.

As you breathe, continue stoking your warmth and light as you inhale, and as you exhale, think to yourself, "May all beings be safe. May all beings be healthy. May all beings be happy." Take several more rounds of breathing as you repeat these phrases and send warmth and light out to all beings.

When you are ready, take an especially deep breath in, and slowly open your eyes.

Myths and Misperceptions about Bullying

> "It takes two to speak the truth—one to speak and the other to hear."—Henry David Thoreau

Objective: Students will explore their own ideas about what it means to be a bully and why people choose to bully others. They will talk about what it might look like to have compassion for someone who is branded a bully.

Tools:

- Discussion Prompt (5–10 minutes of introduction, 20+ minutes of discussion)
- What Does Bullying Look Like? activity (20 minutes)
- Diversity and Community meditation (5 minutes)

Discussion: Ask students to pull out a sheet of paper and answer the following questions on their own. Once everyone is finished, share the answers with them and encourage discussion.

1. True or False: Nearly 40 percent of American teens are involved in bullying. *(True. 13 percent admit bullying others, 21 percent say they've been bullied, and 6 percent say they've experienced both at least once.)*
2. True or False: Most incidents of bullying happen in high school. *(False. Bullying incidents rise sharply beginning in sixth grade and drop off after ninth grade.)*
3. True or False: Schools and communities that are more diverse report more incidents of bullying. *(False. Bullying happens in all communities, but diverse communities that are inclusive and work to promote inclusion have fewer issues with bullying.)*
4. True or False: Students who witness bullying often refuse to remain friends with the victim and feel guilty for not reporting the incident(s). *(True. Witnessing an act of bullying has negative consequences even if a student is not directly involved as the perpetrator or victim.)*
5. True or False: Bullying is about power and control. *(True. While students who bully others often have high self-esteem, their behavior is directed at their own need to be seen as powerful. We tend to shame and strike out at others we think we can control, even if they haven't upset us directly.)*
6. True or False: It should be up to the victim to report and deal with any bullying incidents. *(False. Bullying prevention approaches that show the most promise confront the problem from many angles. They involve the entire school community—students, families, teachers, administrators, and staff, such as bus drivers, nurses, and cafeteria and front office staff—in creating a culture of compassion and respect.)*
7. True or False: Suspension and expulsion are not effective ways to deal with students who bully other students. *(True. These approaches are not helpful in addressing social dynamics in a school community, nor are they effective in helping perpetrators learn to change their behavior over time. Many students who have bullied others and are expelled go on to have criminal convictions as adults.)*

Activity: What Does Bullying Look Like? (see Appendix A)

Meditation: Diversity and Community

As always, allow students ample time to reflect quietly during this meditation.
 Find a comfortable position, and close your eyes. Take a few deep breaths to settle in and clear your mind of any random thoughts. As you relax, picture a computer keyboard in your mind. Can you see all of the letters and numbers

and symbols? Even if the keys all have the same basic shape and their jobs are similar, they look different and have different functions. Each letter of the alphabet, each number, each key with a punctuation mark is important on its own and really powerful when it's used with the other ones.

Imagine that you are one of the symbols—you decide which one. Think about your school papers and email and text messages, think about how they would be different if that symbol didn't exist. Think about how important each one of them is as part of the bigger picture.

Now think about your friends and family and classmates. Each of them is a unique symbol, too, and together you make up a community that is rich and diverse and full of possibility. That is because you are all different. Think about how each individual plays an important role, how you each function on your own, with your own ideas and beliefs and experiences, and how you function together, much of the time pretty comfortably and seamlessly.

Reflect on how vital it is to have each individual performing their role, whatever it may be. Be grateful for the qualities you bring to the table. We are, each of us, important in our own right and, at the same time, part of something larger that both needs us and nourishes us.

When you are ready, take a deep breath, and slowly open your eyes.

What Don't You Know?

> "There is only one thing about which I am certain, and that is that there is very little about which one can be certain."—W. Somerset Maugham

Objective: Students will consider that it is nearly impossible to know all of the details of any situation at first glance. They will examine the ramifications of making decisions and judgments without considering other perspectives and factors.

Tools:

- Discussion Prompt (5–10 minutes of introduction, 20+ minutes of discussion)
- Actor's Nightmare activity (10 minutes)
- Completing the Puzzle meditation (5 minutes)

Discussion: Tell students the following story of a king who assembled several blind men and presented them with an elephant. One at a time, the men were guided to the elephant, stationed at a particular part (front leg, trunk, head, back leg, etc.), and asked to use their hands to explore the animal. When each of the men had thoroughly explored the part of the elephant they were stationed beside, the king asked them each in turn, "What is an elephant?"

The man who had explored the animal's head answered, "An elephant is like a huge pot turned upside down." The man at the ear disagreed, saying, "An elephant is like a huge plant with enormous leaves." The man who had explored the tusk told the king that it was more like a pole while the man who touched the trunk said it was like a giant serpent. They continued on this way, each man describing his own portion of the elephant and, eventually, a heated argument began among them.

Discussion Questions:

- Ask students to discuss the meaning of the parable. Does it illustrate how we each get attached to our own view of the world without considering that there are many more parts we have yet to experience?
- Can anyone recall a time when they were certain of something that they later learned was very different than they originally believed? Has anyone ever vigorously defended a position or belief that they later discovered wasn't entirely accurate?

Activity: Actor's Nightmare (see Appendix A)

Meditation: Completing the Puzzle

As always, be sure to allow students plenty of time to sit quietly and reflect without talking.

Find a comfortable position, and close your eyes gently. Take a few breaths normally to clear any stray thoughts from your head.

When you're ready, imagine a puzzle in your mind that is missing most of the center pieces. The sides and corners are complete, but there are large gaps in the center such that you can't quite determine what the picture is supposed to be. Think about how that feels. Notice how your mind tries to rush ahead and fill in the openings with something that makes sense. Resist that urge as much as possible.

As you trail your imagination around the parts of the puzzle that are complete, notice if that feels different to you. Our brains are wired to fill in gaps with information, even if it isn't absolutely correct. When we do that, we get a surge of dopamine, the feel-good chemical, in our brains. It doesn't matter whether the information is right; it just has to make enough sense to us to feel complete.

Sit for another minute with your eyes closed, and see if you can get more comfortable with not knowing what the full puzzle is supposed to look like. Can you let yourself stop wondering about it?

When you're ready, take a deep breath in, and slowly open your eyes.

Self-Compassion

"If at first you don't succeed, you're about average."—Unknown

Objective: Students will explore the idea of compassion and boundaries and will learn how to have compassion for themselves when they make a mistake.

Tools:

- Discussion Prompt (5–10 minutes of introduction, 20+ minutes of discussion)
- Self-Compassion activity (10 minutes)
- Appreciating Your Body meditation (5 minutes)

Discussion: It is a common misperception that selfishness is the opposite of compassion—that if we are not actively helping someone in need, we are being selfish. In fact, there are many reasons we choose not to reach out to others and some people spend far more time and energy helping others than they do taking care of their own needs. That can be counterproductive, but because helping other people is often praised in some cultures, it can be hard to stop. Sometimes we find ourselves agreeing to something because we think we ought to, even when we don't have the time, energy, or interest. This is when it is important to examine our own boundaries, especially when it comes to relationships with our family and close friends.

Following are some signs of unhealthy boundaries:

- Acting against your values to please someone else
- Letting yourself be defined by someone else
- Sacrificing something for someone else and later resenting it
- Helping someone because you think you "should"
- Overidentifying with someone else's struggle
- Feeling responsible for someone else's emotions

Discussion Questions:

- Have students give examples of unhealthy boundaries and talk about whether they have made these choices before. Has anyone experienced a difficult situation because they didn't have boundaries in place?
- Ask students to think about and perhaps jot down ideas about which people and situations are the most challenging for them when it comes to relationship boundaries. Can they discuss ways to protect themselves by deciding

what they're comfortable with? Can they give themselves permission to say no or redefine boundaries with others?

Activity: Self-Compassion (see Appendix A)

Meditation: Appreciate Your Body

As always, be sure to allow students plenty of time to sit quietly and reflect without talking.

We all spend a lot of time and energy critiquing our bodies. As teenagers, most of us spend a lot of time looking in the mirror, cataloguing the things we would love to change—even just a little bit—and paying more attention to the things we don't like than the things we do. This meditation is designed to give you an appreciation for the things we take for granted every day.

Sit in a comfortable position and close your eyes. Take a few deep breaths in and out to settle in and clear any random stray thoughts you're having. Starting with your feet, think about what they do for you on a daily basis. How they squeeze into shoes or take a beating on hot pavement or sand when you go barefoot. Maybe you play sports and they keep you balanced as the bones and muscles flex to move you in the right direction without you having to think about how that happens. From there, move to your ankles and lower legs.

Think about how the bones support you every day, how blood courses through the veins and arteries to bring nutrients and blood cells, how the old skin sloughs off on its own and new skin is constantly created beneath it automatically. You don't have to tell it when.

Think about the marvel that is your knees, how they bend smoothly to help you squat down and tie your shoe and how they lock into place when you need them to. What about your upper legs? Those powerhouses of muscle and bone that hold you upright, that flex and extend to help you walk and run and skip and ride a skateboard. Your hips? They are amazing, too.

Make your way up your body like this, pausing to be astonished at what happens in your gut all day, every day—hormones and digestive juices being released at the right times, and your food broken down and distributed throughout your body to the places it needs to go without you directing it there. Your kidneys and liver deal with the waste products, and your diaphragm moves to help you breathe. Your lungs exchange gases seamlessly, and your heart beats, beats, beats, and it responds to scary things by speeding up so you can run away if you have to.

Your immune system sends healing cells to make scabs and flush out germs. Your neck holds up your head all day long and twists to help you see what you need to see. Stop and appreciate your arms and hands. Think about how your hair and your fingernails just grow, cells constantly dividing while you're not even aware of it. Acknowledge your ears and eyes and nose and mouth, as well as your brain, for orchestrating all of these complicated and incredibly essential tasks, mostly without your supervision or interference.

Take one more pause to be appropriately awed by your body, and the next time you look in the mirror, give it thanks instead of criticizing it.

When you're ready, take a deep breath in, and open your eyes.

Alternative Forms of Wealth

"Know what you own, and know why you own it."—Peter Lynch

Objective: Students will expand their understanding of the strengths they have to draw on that aren't immediately obvious. They will explore what those reserves are and how they are important in their lives and how to acknowledge them in others as well.

Tools:

- Discussion Prompt (5–10 minutes of introduction, 20+ minutes of discussion)
- Wealth Mapping activity (10–20 minutes)
- Wealth Mapping meditation (5 minutes)

Discussion: Cash is king, right? In large part, that's true, but it's interesting to look at the ways that people have leveraged other forms of wealth to get what they need or want. Human beings have always traded goods and services, and even those without a great deal of material wealth have been able to find opportunities based on their individual skills or talents in many cases.

Modern examples include corporations such as Mercedes-Benz and Dom Pérignon "paying" Instagram personalities for drawing attention to their products by sponsoring parties or giving them goods. However, we can also see folks using their wealth of street smarts or language or natural talent to get their needs met.

Consider the story of Ted Williams, a man who was homeless but had formerly been a radio announcer. Someone heard him asking passersby for money and made a video of him that went viral. He ended up being offered a job and a book deal. It isn't always that striking, but we use our personal wealth in many ways every day, often without really thinking about it.

Some key kinds of wealth we have include:

- Family
- Social capital
- Ability to navigate complex systems
- Willingness to resist
- Language (bi- or trilingual)
- Cultural

Discussion Questions:

- Ask students to consider how these different kinds of assets have impacted their lives. Does anyone have an example of a time when they used one to help themselves or others?
- What does it feel like to think about having a reservoir of wealth such as this? Do students feel more secure in their ability to hold on to these kinds of wealth?
- Have students talk about where these strengths and talents come from and why they are important. Are they as important as money?

Activity: Wealth Mapping (see Appendix A)

Meditation: Wealth Mapping

As always, be sure to allow students plenty of time to sit quietly and reflect without talking.

Find a comfortable seat, and close your eyes. Take a few deep breaths in and out to clear your mind of any random thoughts.

Imagine that you are the center of a wheel, and there are spokes radiating out from you toward other people. Each of these people has wisdom and strength that they've helped you develop. They might be teachers, parents, grandparents, siblings, friends, and so on. You don't have to name them or identify each of them, just take a minute to acknowledge the lines that connect you to them.

These people make up your history, your culture. Maybe they've struggled to give you a better life or taught you something important. Maybe they simply supported you when you were struggling or taught you how to enjoy something that you still love. Imagine energy and wisdom traveling from them to you through the spokes—filling you up so that one day when you need to access information or strength, it is there in reserve. Take a minute to just feel the energy from each of these people going to you.

Think about these reserves as muscles. Every time you use them, they get stronger. Every time you speak up or make your way through a challenge, these forms of wealth grow. Take a minute to express gratitude to those who helped you develop this wisdom. Take another minute to acknowledge yourself for drawing on it and knowing how to use it.

It's important to remember that the life you've led so far has given you an abundance of tools to use as you make your way through the days. Be proud of the wealth you have that is unique to you, and know that using it is an affirmation of your resilience.

When you're ready, take a deep breath, and open your eyes.

NOTE

1. Sivers, Derek. November 2009. "Weird, or just different?" Video retrieved from https://www.ted.com/talks/derek_sivers_weird_or_just_different#t-142839.

Chapter 4

Positive Mindset

EDUCATOR NOTES

Our brains are wired to look for trouble. While this is important in certain situations, it can be hard to overcome the habit of spending more time and energy imagining the negative outcomes of everyday situations than focusing on the positive. We are surrounded by news and media that constantly show us an unbalanced view of the world, which can reinforce the idea that we live in frightening times. The good news is that during adolescence it is possible to help shape our brain's natural tendencies toward fear by looking to the positive parts of our lives with intent.

Recognizing that we are in control of how we see and react to the things around us gives us a sense of power. The more we practice looking for possibilities, the easier it is to see them, and while that doesn't mean ignoring challenges, it can make them more palatable. There is a great deal of evidence that people who are resilient are also grateful and optimistic, so developing techniques and practices for positivity can also help us recover from setbacks more quickly and learn more from them.

LESSONS

Altruism

> "The bond that links your true family is not one of blood, but of respect and joy in each other's life."—Richard Bach

Objective: Students will learn that being generous and kind to others is a great way to cultivate happiness in their own lives. They will explore big and small acts of altruism that they can do every day.

Tools:

- Discussion Prompt (5–10 minutes of introduction, 20+ minutes of discussion)
- Bookend Your Day activity (10 minutes)
- Sharing Joy meditation (5 minutes)

Discussion: The Dictionary.com definition of altruism is "the principle or practice of unselfish concern for or devotion to the welfare of others." There are many ways to do this, and it needn't involve a huge sacrifice on our part. Scientific studies show that generosity makes us feel better, especially when we do something without expecting any kind of recognition or payback. When we see a need that we can fill, no matter how small, and we make an effort to do it, that's altruism. True acts of generosity have a huge positive effect on our self-esteem.

Discussion Questions:

- Have students share everyday examples of altruism from their own lives and talk about how it felt—paying for a younger sibling's ice cream or helping them with their homework or doing a chore at home without being asked. (Try not to give any examples at first and see whether they can identify some on their own.)
- Now talk about something big they did for someone else—maybe walked a 5K to support diabetes research or donated their birthday money to a local charity. How did that feel? Is there a difference between "big" and "little" acts of generosity?
- Ask students whether there is such a thing as an act of generosity that is too small, or does offering a warm smile to a homeless person or a bullied student count? Have them think of ways they can incorporate more acts of altruism into their lives, and challenge them to keep track of such acts for a week to see what that is like.

Activity: Bookend Your Day (see Appendix A)

Meditation: Sharing Joy

Be sure to pause several times throughout the meditation to give students some time to really sit and imagine the ideas in their heads. Ideally, it will last about five minutes.

From time to time, it's important to just stop for a minute and conjure up some happiness. This time, we'll go slowly and sit for about five minutes as we learn how to do this, but anytime during the day when you're feeling low or stressed or catch yourself getting angry, you can take a deep breath and close your eyes for a minute and repeat it quickly. Right now, though, let's close our eyes and breathe deeply a few times to clear our thoughts out.

Now, imagine something that makes you smile—a basket full of puppies, a kitten rolling off the couch, a baby giggling, an actor doing something outrageous on TV, whatever. Once you feel a smile twitching at the corners of your mouth, you've got it.

Without making any noise, I want you to focus on what that feeling is like. Do you feel it in your belly—a laugh getting ready to erupt? Is it warm in your chest or around your mouth? That's happiness.

Next, I want you to imagine that feeling of happiness rippling out into the room, covering everyone and everything in its wake. It might have a color or a sound, or it might just be a wave of energy, but it is powerful, and it radiates out as far as you can see in whatever room you're in. Take a moment to behold its power. You have just shared a joy bomb.

Open your eyes and continue on about your day. Anytime you are feeling a little low, just remember what it felt like to spread that happiness around. Relax and smile for a moment.

Deserving Joy

"Joy is the kind of happiness that doesn't depend on what happens."
—David Steindl-Rast

Objective: Students will learn that they are always deserving of happiness, regardless of the circumstances of their lives or the choices they've made. They will learn how to give themselves permission to experience joy at any time they choose to.

Tools:

- Discussion Prompt (5–10 minutes of introduction, 20+ minutes for discussion)
- Finding Purpose and Meaning activity (10 minutes)
- Cheesecloth/Giant Strainer meditation (5 minutes)

Discussion: Our brains are primed to notice and expect negative, potentially harmful things more than positive things. We remember the bad times in our lives more clearly, and we expect bad things to happen far more often than good things. Especially during our teen years, when the amygdala (controller of the fight/flight/fear response) is in charge.

Often, when something good happens to us, our happy feeling is quickly followed up by a feeling of dread—that either we will lose that thing we just got that makes us happy or that the universe will somehow need to pay us back with something bad to even things out.

Other times, when we feel joy or realize that things are going pretty well for us right now, a sense of guilt seeps in. Who are we to be happy when babies are starving, floodwaters are raging, or friends are suffering?

Sometimes, if we've had trauma in our lives, there is a feeling that we *deserve* happiness, that we have somehow paid our dues by struggling. While that can feel good, it's pretty sad to imagine that we have to earn joy by having difficult times in our lives. Moreover, if you happen to have a pretty chill, pretty happy life right now, it's horrible to think you might pay for it later with lots of trauma.

Discussion Questions:

- Ask students if they have ever worried about being "too happy." Talk about how often they enter a new situation expecting the best outcome as opposed to the worst-case scenario.
- Has anyone ever felt guilty when they were happy because others were unhappy or suffering even if the suffering wasn't something they could control? Discuss that idea. Is it rational?
- Talk about the notion of "deserving joy." Do some people deserve joy more than others? Does your joy take away from someone else's? Is joy like a pie with only a certain amount?
- Talk about the idea of earning joy. What do students think about that? What about joyful little kids—do they have to struggle to earn joy in their lives?

Activity: Finding Purpose and Meaning (see Appendix A)

Meditation: Cheesecloth/Giant Strainer

Explain to students that this meditation is designed to help them release negative energy they have unconsciously collected throughout the day. Whether we are aware of it or not, every time we are around others, we receive their energy. When you walk into a room where two people are arguing, you can feel the tension. We absorb this energy without even realizing it—from the barista who screwed up our drink to the poor homeless man we pass every day on the way to school, the fight we had with a teacher over a missing assignment, or our younger sibling's meltdown right before school. All of this collects in our minds and bodies and weighs us down, but it's not ours to carry. Make sure to pause often and let students imagine the cleansing effect of this meditation.

Close your eyes, and take a few deep breaths to settle in. Imagine a giant piece of cheesecloth (or a giant metal strainer) hovering above your head, and as you breathe slowly and deeply, visualize it making its way through your body, starting at the top of your head and moving down. As it goes, all of the black, sticky negative energy gets caught in it. By the time it has made its way through your neck and arms, torso, hips, legs, and exited the soles of your feet, this strainer is full of every bit of negative energy it found in you. As it moves through your body, you just notice it gathering the negativity—you don't have to catalog every little thing; just let it go, and notice how much lighter and freer you feel as it takes them away. By the end, the only energy left in you is yours, and it looks like a bright, golden light.

If it has been a particularly challenging day, you can shake off the black bits and run the cheesecloth/strainer back up through your feet and body and out the top of your head, collecting any remaining stray bits. Because it is energy and it belongs somewhere, at this point, I tie it up in a bundle and imagine flinging it back out into the universe, where it will find its owner or it is recycled back into something else.

Finding Joy

"When we talk about the glass being half-full or half-empty, we sometimes forget that it's refillable."—Unknown

Objective: Students will explore the idea that joy is something that is always present and learn ways to practice looking for positivity and opportunities to be optimistic.

Tools:

- Discussion Prompt (5–10 minutes of introduction, 20+ minutes of discussion)
- Gratitude Practice activity (10 minutes)
- Wallowing in Happiness meditation (5 minutes)

Discussion: Most of us believe that if we practice certain kinds of things, we can get better at them. Whether it's shooting free throws every day, going over our multiplication tables until we can't stand it anymore, or hitting the skate park after school to work on tricks, we can develop abilities and strengths by doing something over and over again.

What we sometimes have a hard time believing is that the same phenomenon holds true with our brain wiring and emotional health. There is scientific evidence that shows that if you have the same kinds of thoughts and reactions over and over again, it actually begins to shape the pathways of your brain, and when you're a teenager, your brain's ability to be molded in certain ways is stronger than almost any other time in your life.

Gloria Steinem has said, "If you want 'X' at the end of your journey, you have to have 'X' all along the way, too."[1]

What she means is that if you don't live your life in a certain way, by the time you get to your goal, you won't know *how* to live that way. If you want happiness, you have to practice being happy, you have to walk through life finding the good. Many of the people who find great success in their career do so because they enjoyed not only the end result but also the path that got them there as well.

Discussion Questions:

- Ask students to think about things that might be happening in the world right now that would put a smile on their face. Somewhere, there might be puppies wrestling on the floor or a child tasting ice cream for the first time. How does it feel to think about those things?
- Ask students to think about focusing attention on positive things instead of negative ones, even when difficult situations arise. What would it be like if our default setting was happy instead of being on guard for negative experiences?
- What are things they can practice in their lives that could lead to more happiness? Does it make sense to think that you can't have joy at the end if you don't have joy along the way?

Activity: Gratitude Practice (see Appendix A)

Meditation: Wallowing in Happiness

Find a comfortable seat, and close your eyes. Take a few deep breaths in and out to settle in. Let your mind release any nagging thoughts or concerns for right now and relax.

Think of a time when you were at peace. Maybe you were sitting on a riverbank fishing with someone you like or lying in bed on a Saturday morning knowing that you didn't have to get up right away. There could be any number of times, but I want you to picture one, and see if you can feel what that felt like. Imagine the air all around you is the perfect temperature, not too cold or too warm. Your seat is comfortable, or perhaps you're floating on the water. Wherever you are, it is just perfect. Hold that feeling and freeze time. You are the only thing that moves in this moment of happiness and contentment.

Experiment by wiggling your fingers or toes. Shake a leg or an arm and see how the air or the water shimmies around you, enveloping you in this moment of happiness. If you feel like it, let a smile grow on your face and move around more—wallow in this feeling like a pig in mud. This is your moment, your happiness, do what you want with it. Maybe you want to scoop up handfuls and toss them in the air. Perhaps you want to put your face in it and blow bubbles like a kid in the bathtub. Roll around in it, dance in it, play. Spend a few minutes just exploring this expansive feeling of joy however you want to.

When you're done playing, come back to your body here and now and breathe deeply. Remember that feeling of being surrounded by happiness, and imagine it settling into a special place in your brain for the memory. You can access that feeling any time you want to, and you can add to the memories there. The next time you feel content and happy, close your eyes for a moment and tuck that away in your brain. You can find happiness anywhere.

Take one more deep breath, and open your eyes slowly.

Connection

"The only way to have a friend is to be one."—Ralph Waldo Emerson

Objective: People who have more social connections are happier and less likely to struggle with anxiety and depression. Students will learn to think critically about the relationships they choose and the impact those relationships have on them.

Tools:

- Discussion Prompt (5 minutes of introduction, 30+ minutes of discussion)
- The Rule of Five activity (10 minutes)
- Part of the Whole meditation (5 minutes)

Discussion: Solid, healthy relationships are formed between people who feel seen, heard, valued, and not judged. Hopefully, we can all identify people in our lives who treat us that way, and it is important for us to cultivate those relationships in our lives, both by being those people and being around those people. One piece of advice that is often given in regard to developing strong, genuine connections asks us to:

Do Less, Say Less
Listen More, Feel More

Discussion Questions:

- Ask students to take an inventory of the people in their lives who really value them and listen to them. Does it feel as if there are more of these kinds of relationships in their life than other, more shallow ones?
- Encourage students to discuss how often judgment and assumption show up in their close relationships. What does that say about the nature of those connections?
- Ask students to imagine what the most difficult part of practicing the relationship advice discussed here in their existing relationships might be. Are there people with whom it will be easier than others?
- Are there other "rules" or patterns they see when they examine their closest, safest relationships and compare them to others that don't feel genuine or solid?

Activity: The Rule of Five (see Appendix A)

Meditation: Part of the Whole

The text of this meditation is fairly short, so be sure to pause often and leave lots of time for students to reflect as they listen.

Find a comfortable sitting position, and close your eyes. Take a few deep breaths to settle in, and clear your mind of any random thoughts. As you relax, picture a computer keyboard in your mind. Can you see all of the letters and numbers and symbols? Even if the keys all have the same basic shape and their job is similar, they look a little different and have different functions. Each letter of the alphabet and each number, each key that holds a punctuation mark, is important on its own, and really powerful when it is used with the other symbols.

Imagine that you are one of those symbols—you can decide which one if you want to. Think about how your school papers and emails and text messages would be different if that symbol weren't there. Think about how important each one of them is as a part of the bigger picture.

Now think about each of your friends, classmates, and relatives as a unique symbol. Together, you make up a community that is rich and diverse, not because you are all the same, but because you are all different. Think about how each individual plays a key role and how you all function on your own, with your own ideas and beliefs, and how you function together.

Reflect on how vital it is to have each of you performing your own special role, and be grateful for the unique qualities you bring to the table. We are, each of us, important in our own right and part of something larger that both needs us and nourishes us.

When you are ready, take a deep breath, and open your eyes.

The Three Crowns

> "Without leaps of imagination, or dreaming, we lose the excitement of possibilities. Dreaming, after all, is a form of planning."—Gloria Steinem

Objective: Students will explore ideas of competition and self-motivation and talk about the importance of values as they identify their goals and work toward them.

Tools:

- Discussion Prompt (5–10 minutes of introduction, 20+ minutes of discussion)
- Goal-Setting activity (10–20 minutes)
- Saltwater meditation (5 minutes)

Discussion: Steve Wilkinson was a very talented, incredibly successful tennis coach who built a philosophy of coaching on something he called "the three crowns." He explained it like this: "The three crowns focus on things that we can control. The three crowns bring us a stillness of mind." It was perhaps that stillness of mind that led him to such success, even though it didn't focus on scores or a win-loss record but instead the values each player lived by. The crowns are these:

- *Commit to a positive attitude and celebrate what you did well.* Before you ever set foot on the court or in the classroom or anywhere else, promise yourself that you will be positive. You will go in with an open mind, assume that others will have good intentions, and expect a happy outcome. Even if you don't get the outcome you anticipated, look for the strengths. What did you do that demonstrated your skills? Find something positive in your performance.
- *Commit to full effort until the end.* Even if you're going up against an opponent or getting into a situation that you think might be an uphill battle, promise yourself that you will continue to work until it's over. Play as hard as you can until the final buzzer rings. Stay focused on finishing what you started. Even if you're getting blown away, if what you came to do was take this class or play this match or learn this skill, remember to keep working your hardest until it's done.
- *Honor your opponent and be a good sport.* Whether you won or lost, enjoyed the experience or not, there are things you can learn from others. If it was a sporting event, perhaps the other team or player had some moves or techniques you could try. If it was a class, whether you felt like you didn't connect with the instructor personally or you already knew a lot

of the material, there is something in there that was valuable. Find it and appreciate it, and be grateful for the opportunity to learn. It is natural to be disappointed if your expectations weren't met, but that doesn't mean it was a waste. Find the good.

Discussion Questions:

- Ask students to recall a time when a game or event didn't go according to plan. Can they look back and determine the redeeming value of that experience? Perhaps there is more to it than they originally took away from it.
- Talk with students about what it looks like to quit and what it looks like to continue with full effort until the end. Are there situations where this is not possible or worth it?
- Ask students to imagine committing to a positive attitude every single time they try something new (including a sporting event, a school assignment, starting a job, etc.). What are the kinds of things they currently say to themselves in these situations? What kind of a shift in energy and self-talk would it take to be conscious of the three crowns instead?

Remind students that the three crowns are about recognizing what we get to be in control of in any situation. We can't predict or control anyone else's behavior, so to perform at our best and learn from our experiences, we need to focus our attention on what we can do. This philosophy is what led Steve Wilkinson to the all-time best winning record of any tennis coach despite the fact that he never told his players that the goal was to win.

Activity: Goal-Setting (see Appendix A)

Meditation: Saltwater

Sometimes it is hard for us to have perspective on just how a bad day or a rough patch fits into the larger puzzle of our lives. This meditation is designed to give us a little bit of breathing room when we are focused on something negative. Find a comfortable sitting position, and close your eyes. Take a few long, deep breaths in and out to clear any stray thoughts you're having.

When you're ready, I want you to picture a glass of water and a shaker of salt sitting on a counter. The glass of water represents today, and the salt is something unexpected or unhappy. Pick up the salt shaker, and dump some of the salt into the water. Watch as it swirls around and falls to the bottom. Some of it will dissolve, but much of it remains visible in the water. Shake some more in there. Pick up the glass, and twist it back and forth to see the salt move around in the water. Think about how awful it would taste if you took a drink right now. This is what it's like when we are unhappy with the way our day is going.

Take a deep breath and look out a window. You will see a lake outside. Fresh, clean, pure, surrounded by trees. The surface of the lake is still and reflective, and there is a small bench sitting next to it. Pick up the salt shaker and an empty glass, and head out to the bench. Sit down for a minute, and just look at the beautiful lake. The lake is your life. Look at the clear water. Shake some salt into the lake. Watch as it swirls around and falls. Reach in, and stir the water a bit. Wait for it to settle a bit, and dip your glass into the lake to fill it. Hold the glass up to the light and look to see whether you can see any salt crystals in it.

When we are only paying attention to something unhappy that is going on, we are looking at the salt water in the glass. However, if we take the time to remember that the tiny amount of salt doesn't change much when it is compared to a vast lake, we can begin to get perspective on our lives. When I'm having a hard day, I like to remember this quote:

> "On particularly rough days when I'm sure I can't possibly endure, I like to remind myself that my track record for getting through bad days so far is 100 percent, and that's pretty good."—Vinny Genovesi

When you're ready, take a deep breath in, and open your eyes.

Finding Meaning

> "The only way you can make yourself happy is to create a story that will make you happy.... You cannot control what is happening around you, but you can control the way you tell the story."—Unknown

Objective: Students will be asked to identify people they look up to and think about the characteristics they have. They will use this to determine which aspects of people's personalities and behavior are important to them and which they aspire to as a way to think about living a meaningful life.

Tools:

- Discussion Prompt (5–10 minutes of introduction, 20+ minutes of discussion)
- Living a Life of Intent activity (10+ minutes)
- Growth and Change meditation (5 minutes)

Discussion: There are many studies that show that when we don't feel as though we have a purpose or some greater goal, we are more likely to suffer from depression. Animal studies show that they would rather eat food that they have to work for than eat food that is passively available. There is evidence that we value things we make more than we value things that we buy.

It is also important to human beings that our contributions are acknowledged by others. Many of us struggle to define what our purpose might be, and there are some who think that we don't have just one but that throughout our lifetimes we may find many different things meaningful and important.

Ultimately, the life choices we make are guided by the things we find value in. While our activities might change over time, we generally hold on to a similar set of morals throughout our lives, and all of us want to be challenged on some level and feel as though we are doing work that makes a difference to those around us.

Discussion Questions:

- Have students talk about the people they look up to the most. Do those people seem to live with some higher purpose in mind? If there are multiple people a student looks up to, do those people all share some key characteristics?
- What makes a goal "meaningful"? Moreover, how does having a meaningful goal change your attitude toward it, if at all?
- Does anyone currently feel as though they have ideas about what their purpose in life is? Does anyone know how to find that?

Activity: Living a Life of Intent (see Appendix A)

Meditation: Growth and Change

We tend to believe that we can grow and change in certain ways but not in others. For example, you might think that you can get better at baseball or soccer but that you'll always struggle with math or science. The truth is, we are always changing and growing, and as Dr. Shauna Shapiro says, "What you practice grows."[2] This meditation is great for reminding us that we can choose how we see our own growth and that we can always continue to push ourselves to be better at anything.

Sit in a comfortable position, and close your eyes. Breathe deeply in and out a few times to settle in and clear your mind. Picture yourself as a strong, beautiful serpent. Take a minute to look at yourself, note the colors of your scales and the long, strong body. As you breathe deeply, I want you to notice that your current skin is feeling a little too tight, a little restrictive.

Breathe slowly and imagine moving forward, slowly beginning to slither out of that skin and leaving it behind. As you move, sense the restriction easing a bit. Keep progressing a little at a time, and feel the space you have to expand, to become something more, to fully inhabit your new skin.

Once you've fully made your way out of the old shell, look back, and acknowledge how much you've grown. That old skin protected you and shielded you and gave you some of your color for a while, but it's time for you to move on now. You are moving about in the world in a bigger way, with more impact and responsibility. It is normal to feel a little vulnerable before your new skin hardens fully, but you can focus on the freedom and power you have just given yourself. You can choose to shed your old skin anytime it becomes too small. You can move toward the goals you set for yourself, even if it feels frightening, because you deserve to have room to breathe.

NOTES

1. Steinem, Gloria. October 2014. "Wisdom Sharing: A Deepening Retreat." Ghost Ranch, New Mexico.
2. Shapiro, Shauna. March 10, 2017. "The Power of Mindfulness: What you Practice Grows Stronger." Video retrieved from https://www.youtube.com/watch?v=IeblJdB2-Vo.

Chapter 5

Self-Worth

EDUCATOR NOTES

Many adolescents struggle with a sense of self-worth. Our culture is highly competitive, and often, we are faced with impossible standards. Social media platforms offer an unrealistic look at the lives of other adolescents, and even well-meaning adults can place unachievable expectations on adolescents by being quicker to point out areas for growth and improvement than offering praise for hard work and perseverance. When teens hear and see these kinds of messages, they often wonder whether they can ever be good enough.

Adolescence is also a time marked by self-exploration and experimentation with different identities. As students try on different ways of being, it is important that they have a solid foundation of "self" on which to build. These lessons are designed to help them learn about the things that are most important to the student and that make them unique.

LESSONS

Comparison as a Form of Self-Judgment

> "Self-love has very little to do with how you feel about your outer self. It's about accepting all of yourself."—Tyra Banks

Objective: Students are taught to become aware of how often they compare themselves to others and how this impacts their feelings of self-worth. They will learn to identify examples of comparison in their daily lives and talk about ways to mitigate the effects of judgment on how they see themselves.

Tools:

- Discussion Prompt (5–10 minutes of introduction, 20+ minutes of discussion)
- What Makes You Unique? activity (10+ minutes)
- Appreciating Your Body meditation (5 minutes)

Discussion: Let's talk about judgment. How often do you size yourself up when you walk in a room—generally without even realizing you're doing it? How many times do you rethink your hairstyle or outfit in the morning? Is it fairly common for you to compare what you said in class to what someone else said? Do you mentally beat yourself up because you think you could have been smarter/funnier/quicker? Do you sometimes gloat because you see yourself as better looking or more athletic or more popular than other kids?

Our brains are designed to judge situations and people, and unless we take the time to stop and recognize that we're doing it and assess whether it is actually useful in any given situation, it gets more and more automatic. It becomes the backdrop of everything we do, despite the fact that the purpose of judgment is to discern whether a situation is safe for us. What we've evolved to do is turn that judgment on ourselves, and it becomes destructive to our sense of self.

Discussion Questions:

- Ask students to talk about what it feels like to judge and be judged. Are the two feelings different? How would students describe each feeling?
- Prompt students to calculate how often in any given day they see and hear people being compared to each other. Can they cite examples at home, at school, and in the media? What about literature or sports?
- Can students identify places where they can just be who they are without being judged? What is it about those places that make them so easy to be in? What would it take to create more safe places like that, both for themselves and others?

Activity: What Makes You Unique? (see Appendix A)

Meditation: Appreciate Your Body

We all spend a lot of time and energy critiquing our bodies. As teenagers, most of us spend a lot of time looking in the mirror, cataloging the things we would love to change—even just a little bit—and paying more attention to the things we don't like than the things we do. This meditation is designed to give you an appreciation for the things we take for granted every day.

Sit in a comfortable position and close your eyes. Take a few deep breaths in and out to settle in and clear any random stray thoughts you're having.

Starting with your feet, think about what they do for you on a daily basis. How they squeeze into your shoes or take a beating on hot pavement or sand when you go barefoot. Maybe you play sports and they keep you balanced as the bones and muscles flex to move you in the right direction without you having to think about how that happens. From there, move to your ankles and lower legs.

Think about how the bones support you every day, how blood courses through the veins and arteries to bring nutrients and blood cells, how the old skin sloughs off on its own and new skin is constantly created beneath it automatically. You don't have to tell it when.

Think about the marvel that is your knees, how they bend smoothly to help you squat down and tie your shoe and how they lock into place when you need them to. What about your upper legs? Those powerhouses of muscle and bone that hold you upright, that flex and extend to help you walk and run and skip and ride a skateboard. Your hips? They are amazing, too.

Make your way up your body like this, pausing to be astonished at what happens in your gut all day, every day—hormones and digestive juices being released at the right times, and your food is broken down and distributed throughout your body to the places it needs to go without you directing it there. Your kidneys and liver deal with the waste products, and your diaphragm moves to help you breathe. Your lungs exchange gases seamlessly, and your heart beats, beats, beats, and it responds to scary things by speeding up so you can run away if you have to.

Your immune system sends healing cells to make scabs and flush out germs. Your neck holds up your head all day long and twists to help you see what you need to see. Stop and appreciate your arms and hands. Think about how your hair and your fingernails just grow, cells constantly dividing while you're not even aware of it. Acknowledge your ears and eyes and nose and mouth, as well as your brain, for orchestrating all of these complicated and incredibly essential tasks, mostly without your supervision or interference.

Take one more pause to be appropriately awed by your body, and the next time you look in the mirror, give it thanks instead of grief.

Shame

> "Shame is the most powerful master emotion. It's the fear that we're not good enough."—Brené Brown

Objective: Students will explore ideas of shame and learn about the difference between shame and responsibility. They will talk about how shame impacts the way they see themselves and share strategies for combating and resisting it.

Tools:

- Discussion Prompt (5–10 minutes of introduction, 20+ minutes of discussion)
- Self-Compassion Inventory activity (10 minutes)
- Combating Shame meditation (5 minutes)

Discussion: Brené Brown is a researcher at the University of Houston who studies shame and its impact on us. One of her most important findings about shame is that it often shows up when we identify with our actions too much. For example, if I am caught lying and that leads to the belief that I am a "liar," that is shame. If instead I acknowledge that I am a good person who made the mistake of lying, that is taking responsibility for my actions but not allowing myself to be defined by them.

Taking responsibility for a mistake or poor decision allows me to accept that failure, move on, and learn from it. Believing that I am a "liar" or a "cheater" means that I have given up on learning because I am already resigned to the fact that I'm a bad person in some way.

Discussion Questions:

- Have students discuss this idea of shame versus responsibility and talk about times when they have fallen into the trap of letting themselves (even just for a little while) be defined by their worst mistake. Can they see whether there were ripple effects from that?
- Can students identify people in their lives whose words or actions seem to trigger this kind of shame-thinking in them?
- How many students are adept at shaming themselves, even if someone else doesn't point out a mistake they made? Can they identify the kinds of phrases they use when they do this?

Activity: Self-Compassion Inventory (see Appendix A)

Meditation: Combating Shame

Shame is destructive and corrosive. It eats us from the inside out, and it convinces us that we are not smart, capable, lovable people. We all know what shame feels like, but how do we shake it off? This can help.

Find a comfortable sitting position, and close your eyes. Take a few deep breaths in and out to settle in and release any random thoughts you might be having.

Try to remember a time when you felt shame. Without getting sucked into the story, focus on what it felt like in your body. For some people, shame is hot—our faces flush, our stomachs tighten and burn. Some people shrink into a fetal position. Pretend you're an innocent bystander and just notice the reactions your body has to shame. Don't hold on to them or build a story around them.

It is important to know that as long as we don't grasp the physical effects of emotion or try to fight them, they peak and disappear within about ninety seconds. If we resist the urge to let our mind build a story around them with memories or judgment, we can let them come and go like a wave on the beach.

Picture yourself sitting cross-legged on the beach just at the spot where the waves break on shore. Sit with your back to the ocean, which means you don't know when the next wave is coming or how big it will be. Don't be afraid. These waves are small and calm, they might barely touch your back, or they might come up as far as your shoulder blades, but you are safe. Just sit there, and allow the waves to crash into you and recede. This is what it is like when you let emotions come and go without fighting them. Sit there for a minute and let some small and big waves wash over your back and retreat back out to sea.

Now practice conjuring up different emotions, and let them do the same. Think of a time when you were frustrated with someone. Remember what that felt like in your body, and let it go. Think of a time when you were incredibly sad, and recognize what that felt like in your body. Let it go. Watch a few more feelings wash over you and move on—try anger and fear. Let them go.

The last feeling you'll think of is shame. Let it come and go. Let it come and go again. Remind yourself that your emotions don't define you and they don't control you. They visit and go away if you let them, leaving behind a clear, smooth beach where you can write any story you choose.

When you're ready, take a deep, cleansing breath, and open your eyes.

Fitting In

"The reward for conformity is that everyone likes you but yourself."—Rita Mae Brown

Objective: Students will explore ideas of individuality and contrast them against the desire to be part of something bigger than themselves. They will talk about whether it is possible to be part of a community without compromising their own values and unique qualities.

Tools:

- Discussion Prompt (5–10 minutes of introduction, 20+ minutes of discussion)
- Authentic People and Values activity (10–20 minutes)
- Part of the Whole meditation (5 minutes)

Discussion: We are all adept at looking at ourselves through different lenses depending on the context. Home might feel "normal" until you think about inviting a friend over whose family has more money than yours. At that point, the furnishings and neighborhood might seem embarrassing and inadequate—something you have to hide or apologize for.

As you get older, you might be perfectly comfortable with your housekeeping skills until your mother or father wants to come for a visit. All of a sudden, you can see the cat hair and try to remember the last time you washed the towels in the bathroom.

As an adult, the thought of inviting your boss over for dinner or having your in-laws come to stay for a few days could throw you into a spiral of fear, despite the fact that you have friends over all the time and that seems just fine.

By the time we are in our teens, most of us have gotten really good at sizing up social situations and determining who we need to be as we enter. We quickly figure out how to conform or fit into that particular room, and it can leave us feeling a little empty or fake.

Some teens have particular talents that they loathe sharing because they don't want to stand out—either to be the center of attention or to seem as if they're showing off. However, that sense that we need to be more like our peers than distinct from them can keep us from really exploring the opportunities we could have. We all want to be part of something bigger than ourselves—especially during the teen years when we are pulling away from parents and forging new relationships—but when we get scared that we aren't smart/athletic/pretty/strong enough, we can falter, and it is often more frightening to think about being shunned from a group than it is to express who we really are.

Discussion Questions:

- Ask students to talk about how the need to "fit in" shows up in their lives. Has it ever kept anyone from doing something they wished later they'd done?
- Ask students to talk about the difference between "fitting in" and "belonging." Do those states of being feel different?
- Is it possible to belong to a group of friends without liking all of the same things those people like? Does anyone have examples of that? What happens when you express your unique perspective instead of simply agreeing with everyone else?

Activity: Authentic People and Values (see Appendix A)

Meditation: Part of the Whole

Find a comfortable sitting position, and close your eyes. Take a few deep breaths to settle in and clear your mind of any random thoughts. As you relax, picture a computer keyboard in your mind. Can you see all of the letters and numbers? Even if the keys all have the same basic shape and their job is similar, they look a little different and have different functions. Each letter of the alphabet and each number, each key that holds a punctuation mark, is important on its own, and really powerful when it is used with the other symbols.

Imagine that you are one of those symbols—you can decide which one if you want to. Think about how your school papers and emails and text messages would be different if that symbol wasn't there. Think about how important each one of them is as a part of the bigger picture.

Now think about all of your friends, classmates, and relatives as a unique symbol. Together, you make up a community that is rich and diverse, and that is not because you are all the same, but because you are all different. Think about how each of the individuals plays a key role and how you all function on your own, with your own ideas and beliefs, and how you function together. Reflect on how vital it is to have each of you performing your own special role and be grateful for the unique qualities you bring to the table. We are, each of us, important in our own right and part of something larger that both needs us and nourishes us.

When you are ready, take a deep breath, and open your eyes.

Platonic Ideals

"When you stop expecting people to be perfect, you can like them for who they are."—Donald Miller

Objective: Students will talk about the notion of "perfect" or "ideal" and see how subjective those notions are. They will discuss the purpose and examine the assumptions they make about themselves in an effort to be more accepting of their flaws and talents.

Tools:

- Discussion Prompt (5–10 minutes of introduction, 20+ minutes of discussion)
- Stories I Tell Myself activity (10–20 minutes)
- Changeable Me meditation (5 minutes)

Discussion: The ancient philosopher Plato had an idea known as the Theory of Forms, which basically says that each object that belongs to a particular group of objects (regardless of what it looks like in reality) contains some ideal set of characteristics that makes it part of that group. For example, there are many different types of chairs, but there is something about each one of them (plush ones and wooden ones alike) that we recognize as chair-like.

He said that there is some essential set of qualities that give them each a chair-ness.

This concept is sometimes called "Platonic Idealism," and over time, in some cultures, the concept has morphed into the notion that there is one "ideal" form of everything. While Plato was simply exploring ideas of form and shape and function, human beings often use ideas like his to assert some belief about perfection or the "best" form of something, such as the human body.

Discussion Questions:

- Ask students to discuss this idea and how it shows up in their lives and the way they feel about themselves. Is there an "ideal" body type? Or an "ideal" skin tone or accent or set of qualities that a teenage girl or boy ought to have?
- Have students explore whether there is truly an "ideal" form of anything. Perhaps one chair is ideal in one situation but not in another (If your classroom was populated with recliners, would much learning take place? Does anyone want to watch TV or play video games in a hard, wooden chair?).
- Have students make a list of their own ideal qualities (they don't have to share them if they don't want to). Do they think their list differs from their classmates' lists? Do the qualities change depending on what they are doing on any given day? Is that OK?

Activity: Stories I Tell Myself (see Appendix A)

Meditation: Changeable You

Find a comfortable sitting position, and close your eyes. Take a few deep breaths in and out to settle in and release any random thoughts you're having.

Try to remember what you looked like when you were a baby. Maybe you had a lot of hair; maybe you were bald. If you can, recall a photo of what you looked like at the time, and take a minute to observe it closely. When you are ready, try to picture yourself as you are now, maybe even conjure up a memory of your most current school picture and set it right next to your baby picture in your mind. There are some things that have remained the same—maybe your eye color or skin tone, but a lot has changed since then.

You will continue to change and develop throughout your life, but even though the things other people see are shifting and growing, the real you is still there. Try to see if you can identify a part of you that is YOU and imagine where it is. Maybe it's hidden deep in your belly, or perhaps you feel it in your chest near your heart, or maybe it is in your brain. There is no right or wrong place because it's you.

Now focus on those photos of you and place a bright, golden spot in the area where you feel your personal essence on each picture. This is a reminder that no matter what other people see, no matter how you change over time, there is something that just defines you as you, making you special and unique.

Your abilities have gotten stronger over the years, too. You are much better at walking now than you were as a baby, I bet. Moreover, throughout your lifetime, you will both gain and lose abilities, and yet you will still be yourself. Imagine what you might look like at age fifty, and place that picture right next to the others in your mind. Look at the physical changes and similarities for a moment. Then see if you can determine what it is that links all of these photos together. Feel what it is that makes you always and forever you. That part is impervious to change, immune to time.

When you are ready, stack the photos, and breathe deeply. Take one last look at the golden light, and open your eyes.

Pressure to Perform

> "We may encounter many defeats, but we must not be defeated."—Maya Angelou

Objective: Students will examine the ways in which external expectations and pressures affect the way they feel about themselves. They will go deeper in their personal reflections on shame and how it affects them.

Tools:

- Discussion Prompt (5–10 minutes of introduction, 20+ minutes of discussion)
- Shame Progression activity (10 minutes)
- Leaves in a Stream meditation (5 minutes)

Discussion:

> "Over the years, I have learned that we humans tend to be happier when we are where we belong rather than trying to get somewhere that is not really who we are."—Daniel Gottlieb

Often, when we are feeling anxious, it is because we are afraid that we can't live up to some external expectation. When we are internally motivated to accomplish something, we are more able to overcome mistakes and keep pushing through obstacles because the end result is something that we have decided is important to us.

When we are trying to do something that we think will make others like us better or look on us favorably, we get our own self-worth tied up with what we think others value about us. When we use outside standards to determine how we feel about ourselves, we can't ever really be comfortable with who we are, because those standards could change quickly and then we're left playing catch-up.

It has also been shown that the more we try to change ourselves, the more our focus narrows. The more self-critical we are, the more self-absorbed we are. That means that we are less able to accurately predict what others are thinking about us, even though we trick ourselves into believing that they really are judging us.

Discussion Questions:

- Ask students to talk about a time when they did something to please someone else. What did that feel like in the short term? What did it feel like in the long term?
- What kinds of pressure do students feel to live up to external expectations? Where does that pressure come from? How can they address it in their lives?

Activity: Shame Progression (see Appendix A)

Meditation: Leaves in a Stream

Close your eyes and take some slow, deep breaths in and out through your nose. Try to empty your brain of all thought and realize how hard it is to do that. Even if you can manage it for a minute or two, it's normal for our brains to get sucked back in to reacting to something you hear or how your seat feels or worrying about an assignment or test you have tomorrow. It's pretty rare for anyone to be able to empty their head of all thought for very long, but this visualization can keep you from getting caught up in them for a few minutes and give your brain a rest.

Imagine you are sitting near a stream. Take a minute to picture the surroundings—maybe it's a shady forest or a sunny meadow. The stream can be wide or thin, deep or shallow, loud and gurgling or quiet. There is something large nearby that you can lean against—a rock or tree or bench. Sit for a minute and flesh out the scene.

Every time you have a thought, imagine it as a leaf falling from a nearby tree and slowly fluttering down to land in the water. As it comes into your line of sight—as you have the thought—notice it, watch it land, and see it float downstream from you. Don't chase it. Don't name it. Just notice it, and let it go.

There may be times when you have fifty thoughts in a minute and others when there are only a few, or one at a time. Let them all go. They are leaves in a stream. Sit for a minute and practice watching them go without describing them. Just notice.

When you're ready, take a very deep breath through your nose, and open your eyes.

Chapter 6

Stress, Anxiety, and Fear

EDUCATOR NOTES

Stress, anxiety, and fear are overwhelming for many adolescents. Even for those who are not debilitated by it, it can be a constant challenge to overcome the messages they receive to be better, stronger, and smarter. Unfortunately, fear and stress impair our ability to learn and our willingness to be curious and explore the world, and during this time of dramatic brain development, it is important to keep our children learning.

Stress and anxiety are often responses to our culture's thirst for academic achievement; teen suicide rates are higher than ever, there is more competition to get into "good" colleges, and kids spend more time doing extracurricular activities than ever before.

While these lessons and activities are by no means a substitute for counseling, they can help teens and tweens gain a little more insight into how stress and anxiety affect their lives and how to handle it a little better. Adolescents who are suffering from anxiety often report feeling isolated and ashamed, and discovering how many of their peers struggle with similar feelings can be a great comfort.

Many individuals who struggle with stress, anxiety, and fear believe that these things are simply characteristics they will have forever; however, we can learn new ways to think about and cope with these uncomfortable emotions and realize that we are not defined by them. Developing an understanding of how stress, anxiety, and fear show up in our lives is the first step toward learning how to manage these emotions instead of being held hostage by them. By acknowledging that these are common feelings, students can move through them rather than fighting or denying them and begin to anticipate when they might show up. Over time, they will build resilience. In this section, they will learn how each emotion works and how to handle them.

LESSONS

Going It Alone

> "STRESS = **S**omeone **T**rying to **R**epair **E**very **S**ituation **S**olo."—Dave Willis

Objective: Students will learn about the positive effects of sharing their feelings and frustrations and discover that doing so can strengthen relationships rather than put them in jeopardy.

Tools:

- Discussion Prompt (5 minutes of introduction, 20+ minutes of discussion)
- Short-Circuit the Anxiety Reaction activity (10 minutes)
- Digging Out meditation (5 minutes)

Discussion: Human beings are social creatures. We live in communities for a reason, namely, that nobody is equipped to tackle every challenge alone. Ever since humans have existed, we have collaborated in order to make our lives better. Studies show that people with more social connections have fewer depressive symptoms as well. What if the beauty of challenges is that they offer us opportunities to work with and more deeply connect with others?

Discussion Questions:

- Ask students to think about their closest, most cherished relationships. Were any of them forged after one person needed help and the other one gave it? The people we trust most in life are often the ones who saved our bacon a time or two or those whose bacon we saved.
- Talk with students about how they react when friends or family members are struggling. Do they have compassion and empathy, or do they blame them and talk down to them? How is that different than the way they talk to themselves when they find themselves in a jam? If it is different, why?
- Why are many of us so determined to take care of our problems alone and keep them quiet? What would it take for us to see our mistakes as learning opportunities or potential ways to connect more authentically with others?

Activity: Short-Circuit the Anxiety Reaction (see Appendix A)

Meditation: Digging Out

Sometimes things happen that we have no control over, and they cause us trauma. It is important to know that our brains treat all trauma the same way; whether it's abuse, a car accident, the death of someone close to you—your brain just imprints it as trauma. Some people have more effective ways of dealing with the aftereffects of trauma, but it is never OK to compare your trauma with anyone else's, either to belittle theirs or to try and talk yourself out of feeling sad and scared ("Seriously, why is my parents' divorce bugging me so much? It isn't like someone died!"). You don't have to make excuses for how you feel.

Find a comfortable sitting position, and close your eyes. Take a few deep breaths to settle in and clear any stray thoughts. Picture yourself waking up in a small house. It's cozy and warm and the middle of winter. As you walk to the kitchen, you look outside and notice there was a blizzard overnight, and you are stuck inside the house. All you can see outside is white—piles and piles of snow. When you listen to the radio, you realize this isn't going to thaw anytime soon, and if you want to get anywhere, it's up to you to do something about it.

This is your trauma. You can absolutely stay inside and hope for rescue, or you can pick up a shovel and start digging a path.

The important thing to know about this snowstorm/trauma is that it isn't your fault. You didn't do anything to create it or ask for it, but you're stuck with it for now. If you want to get out, you're going to have to start working. It may take days and lots of effort on your part, but you can make progress every time you work on it. Even better, you can imagine someone into being who will help you. Think about someone you trust, who loves you, and who won't yell at you about the mess.

Dress warmly and comfortably, and when you're ready, you and your helper can both pick up a snow shovel and open the door.

There is just enough room to scoop up some snow and put it to the side. Each time you dig in, you are acknowledging some of the pain you feel. Work as quickly or as slowly as you wish. You are welcome to take breaks and come inside where it's warm to relax. You've got a companion or companions who make the work lighter. Working on it nonstop will wear you out, and you'll only have to spend more time recovering. With every scoop, know that you are making the piles smaller.

Take a break and come inside. Do something that feels restful and nourishing. Acknowledge what it feels like to know that someone is there to help you when you're ready to begin again, and then take a minute to feel good about the work you've done, including asking for help. When you're feeling settled and rested, take a deep breath, and open your eyes.

Fear, Wisdom, and Equanimity

> "Don't believe every worried thought you have. Worried thoughts are notoriously inaccurate."—Renee Jain

Objective: Students will learn that it is the way they view the world that has the most impact on their mood and emotions. They will explore ideas about fear and changing perspective and talk about the choices they make every day that affect their outlook.

Tools:

- Discussion Prompt (5–10 minutes of introduction, 20+ minutes of discussion)
- Cracking Up Your Inner Critic activity (10 minutes)
- Being in Your Body meditation (5 minutes)

Discussion: Fear is a great survival tool but only when used with some perspective. When we are afraid, we are looking to the future to see what *might* go wrong. Unfortunately, all too often we convince ourselves that these predictions are the likely outcome when they generally aren't. It turns out that our worst fears rarely come true, but our brains are hardwired to expect the worst so that we can try to plan for it. It's important, during the adolescent years, to try and mitigate some of that anxiety by enacting a little rewiring and putting emphasis on learning from past experiences.

Wisdom looks to the future, but it also takes into account what has happened in the past, and when it looks forward, it sees possibility instead of tragedy. When we don't get caught up in the emotions of fear, we can begin using wisdom instead. When we can remind ourselves that happy endings do occur, we can talk ourselves down from some of that fear and anxiety.

Equanimity is a word that means simply accepting where you find yourself right now without building a story around it. It doesn't say, "Man, why am I here again?" and it also doesn't say, "Oh, dang! This is gonna be bad." It simply says, "I forgot to turn in my math assignment. Crud."

In *Learning from the Heart*, Daniel Gottlieb writes about his dad in a perfect illustration of how our mindset can color our expectations. His father got older and progressively lost his hair, as well as "his hearing, his stamina and his sense of taste. Losing those things didn't seem to bother him much, but some other things did. When he was in his eighties, my father used to say, 'I'm ready to leave this vale of tears.' One day I asked him if he was really in so much emotional pain that he was ready to die. 'Some days, I am,' he said. 'So tell me about those days, Dad.' 'Well, I get thinking. I buried my wife and my daughter. And I think of my only son struggling every day in a wheelchair. Those days I'm ready to die.' 'But Dad,' I said, 'those things are true every day. What about those days you aren't ready to die?' He thought about it for a minute. 'I guess I'm not thinking about those things on those days.'"[1]

Discussion Questions:

- Ask your students to think about a time when they worried about the worst-case scenario and it didn't happen. What did it feel like to be consumed by fear? How did it feel later when their worst fear didn't come to pass?
- Ask students whether they have days when they struggle with the circumstances of their lives more than others. Can they identify any patterns? For instance, could it be on the days when their glass is "half full" that they are busy doing things they enjoy?
- Have your students identify a short list of things in their lives that they can't control that they sometimes get upset about. Ask them to talk about strategies for accepting those things and creating more days where they can let go and have more equanimity.

Activity: Cracking Up Your Inner Critic (see Appendix A)

Meditation: Being in Your Body

Some students who have suffered physical trauma may choose to opt out of this meditation because it can bring up reserves of emotion that are uncomfortable. If at any time a student expresses their discomfort with being in their body, the feeling should be honored.

Find a comfortable sitting position, and breathe deeply in and out. Notice whether your belly moves or not. If most of your breath is in your chest, try to see if you can get your belly to move more than your chest. This often results in deeper breaths.

Continue breathing deeply and slowly, and focus on your left foot. Notice what it feels like, and see if you can picture it in your mind's eye. Slowly move your attention up your left leg to your hip as you breathe in, and as you exhale, slide your attention back down to your foot. Notice whether you feel anything in that leg. Are there any areas of tightness or discomfort? Any sensations you notice? Keep breathing.

Now focus your awareness on your right foot. Pay close attention for a moment before you slide your breath up and down your right leg. At first, you're just breathing in and out, and after the first round, you can note whether you feel anything significant. Don't name anything or label it bad or good; just notice it and move on.

Now focus on your stomach. Feel it rise as you breathe in and sink as you exhale. Notice any sensation in your belly as you breathe in and out slowly a few times.

Move your attention to your left hand, and really feel how it is. What is it resting on? Is it flat or curled a little? Breathe in, and move your focus up your arm and through your elbow to the shoulder. Breathe out, and scan your attention back down. Breathe for two more rounds up and down, noticing any sensations present.

Repeat this with your right hand. Breathe in and out, and stay with your hand. Breathe in as you move up your arm and out as you move down. Do two more rounds with focused attention on anywhere that feels different.

Breathe deeply and notice your lungs filling and emptying. Focus your attention up through your neck to your face. Slowly breathe into your jaw, and relax your throat. See if you can relax your facial muscles completely. Breathe as you pay attention to your ears, the back of your head, and the top of your head. Breathe for a few rounds, and note whether you feel any tension or discomfort anywhere.

Lastly, you'll breathe deeply, moving your attention from the soles of your feet up through your body and out the top of your head. Relax, and open your eyes.

How We Freak Ourselves Out

"Don't ruin a good today by thinking about a bad yesterday."—Unknown

Objective: Students will learn about the progression of thoughts to feelings that result in anxiety and stress. They will explore ways to build awareness and begin practicing ways to see everyday situations indifferently.

Tools:

- Discussion Prompt (5–10 minutes of introduction, 20+ minutes of discussion)
- Dealing with Social Anxiety activity (10 minutes)
- Growth and Change meditation (5 minutes)

Discussion: By the time we are in our teen years, we are pretty good at freaking ourselves out, whether we know it or not. One way we do so is by saying to ourselves, "I should(n't) have _____" or "I can't _____" as we think about what someone else would have expected us to do. We do this so automatically that we are generally pretty far down the road of anxiety before we realize it, if we realize it at all.

We believe our thoughts and assumptions, and when we start to act on them, we can build habits that last for a long time. Maybe you are invited out to lunch with a group of friends and you want to go, but you don't have any money to spend. A typical thought process can go something like this:

1. If I ask someone to loan me money, they'll think I'm poor and not invite me to come again.
2. If they think I'm poor, they will either pity me and treat me differently or avoid me because it's so awkward.
3. If I act like I'm not hungry, I don't have to worry about any of that.

The third solution seems perfectly reasonable until the next time you're invited to join these same friends again. If your strategy worked the first time, you'd likely tell everyone that you're not hungry again. What ends up happening is that you set a pattern of behavior and interaction with friends based on your assumptions and fear, and you end up being hungry and watching them all as they eat.

We spend a lot of time and energy imagining that we know what other people are thinking about us without actually checking any of it out. These imaginings are almost always driven by fear and make us feel awful about ourselves. Missing that layup in PE can make us feel as if everyone in the room is laughing at us, but that is rarely the case, and even if they do, they've likely moved on during the next minute or two, but that feeling of embarrassment stays with us for hours or days afterward. The amount of time that others are thinking about us is generally much smaller than the amount of time we believe they are.

Discussion Questions:

- Have students think of a time when they made a decision based on the assumption that others would judge them. Can they look at the thought process and determine how their behavior was affected by this assumption?
- Ask students to talk about a time when they made a mistake that other people witnessed. Talk about what that felt like and how long the emotion persisted. Now ask students how often they really think about the everyday actions of other people during the course of a day.
- How often are students harsher critics of themselves than they are of others? Can they try to be as patient with themselves as they are with their best friend or a younger sibling?
- Discuss whether there are similarities in the kinds of things that send students into an anxiety spiral of negative or fearful self-talk. Are they all worried about the same things, for the most part?

Activity: Dealing with Social Anxiety (see Appendix A)

Meditation: Growth and Change

We tend to believe that we can grow and change in certain ways but not in others. For example, you might think that you can get better at baseball or soccer but that you'll always struggle with math or science. The truth is, we are always changing and growing, and as Dr. Shauna Shapiro says, "What you practice grows."[2] This meditation is great for reminding us that we can choose how we see our own growth and that we can always continue to push ourselves to be better at anything.

Sit in a comfortable position, and close your eyes. Breathe deeply in and out a few times to settle in and clear your mind. Picture yourself as a strong, beautiful serpent. Take a minute to look at yourself, and note the colors of your scales and the long, strong body. As you breathe deeply, I want you to notice that your current skin is feeling a little too tight, a little restrictive.

Breathe slowly and imagine moving forward, slowly beginning to slither out of that skin and leaving it behind. As you move, sense the restriction easing a bit. Keep progressing a little at a time and feel the space you have to expand, to become something more, to fully inhabit your new skin.

Once you've fully made your way out of the old shell, look back and acknowledge how much you've grown. That old skin protected you and shielded you and gave you some of your color for a while, but it's time for you to move on now. You are moving about in the world in a bigger way, with more impact and responsibility. It is normal to feel a little vulnerable before your new skin hardens fully, but you can focus on the freedom and power you have just given yourself. You can choose to shed your old skin anytime it becomes too small. You can move toward the goals you set for yourself, even if it feels frightening, because you deserve to have room to breathe.

When you're ready, take an especially deep breath in, and open your eyes.

The Power of Story

> "Some people expend tremendous energy merely to be normal."
> —Albert Camus

Objective: Students will become aware of how often we all rely on individual stereotypes to define ourselves and begin to find ways to break out of those boundaries to really express their complex personalities.

Tools:

- Discussion Prompt (5–10 minutes of introduction, 20+ minutes of discussion)

- Calming Physical Reactions to Anxiety activity (10 minutes)
- Walking the Path meditation (5 minutes)

Discussion: Human beings love stories. We find them both entertaining and useful for organizing information. Unfortunately, when the same stories are told over and over again, they often become exaggerated and lose some of their "truth," but we still believe them and live our lives as if they are real. Are you the "fearless one"? The "control freak"? The "ditz"? There may be several examples of how you exhibit some of those characteristics, but as we grow and age, we often cling to those old stories instead of recognizing all of the other things that we do or say or care about that might not fit that story anymore.

It is important to note that we all do this, and it is rarely done with bad intent. It is normal for us to find shorthand ways to describe our friends and family, and often, we find it humorous as well. The trouble comes when we start to believe that those things tell the whole story of who we are.

However, what about the stories we wish people told about us? Do you hope people see you as generous and openhearted or ambitious and driven? When we feel like the more negative stories are taking over, it can help to mentally list a couple of examples of things that defy those stories to shift our perspective and ensure that we don't get trapped into habits of conforming to others' ideas of us.

Discussion Questions:

- Have students share some of the stories told about them in their family or friend groups. Is it harmful or helpful to let those labels define them? Is it limiting at all?
- Has anyone ever used those stories or labels to justify their action or inaction in a particular scenario?
- What is one story you wish was told about you that isn't?

Activity: Calming Physical Reactions to Anxiety (see Appendix A)

Meditation: Walking the Path

Find a comfortable position, and close your eyes softly. Take a deep breath to clear any stray thoughts from your mind.

Imagine that you are entering a brightly lit building, and once inside, you see several paths stretching out in front of you. There is no rush to choose one, so you can stand and observe as long as you want to. Signs are pointing to different areas where you can dance and sing, where you can choose to spend time quietly reading, where you can join loved ones, or pursue activities that are important to you, such as sports or gaming or art.

As you begin to move down one path, signs from the paths you didn't choose flash in front of you from time to time and side routes open up as possibilities. You can decide whether to shift your path or not at any time. If you feel you've chosen a path that isn't really fitting anymore, create a new one in your imagination to step onto. Name it. Notice what it feels like, what you think about as you step onto it. Take a minute to think about how you decide which path is the "correct" one for right now.

Stop for a minute and see if you can decide what one of your most deeply held values is. Is it family or hard work? Creativity or social justice? Rest or laughter? When you have one key value in your head, imagine a path opening up before you that nurtures that value and lets you move forward.

See all of the other signs fall away as you take a few steps forward, and think about what it feels like to be on this path that represents your true self and something that is incredibly important to you. Sit with that feeling for a minute before taking another deep breath and opening your eyes.

Rewiring the Brain to Chill

"The fears we don't face become our limits."—Robin Sharma

Objective: Students will learn to identify when they are beginning to get anxious and work on ways to keep their anxiety from taking over.

Tools:

- Discussion Prompt (5–10 minutes of introduction, 20+ minutes of discussion)
- Relaxation Strategies activity (10 minutes)
- Change as a Constant meditation (5 minutes)

Discussion: Our nervous systems are wired to perk up when we encounter someone or something unusual. This can be anything from an unexpected sound or shadow to a situation where we don't see anyone who looks like us to a disapproving look on the face of a parent or teacher.

When this happens, we feel many things—our heart rate quickens, we can break out in a sweat, and our hands might get cold. We start breathing faster, and our muscles tense up. All of these things are biologically designed to help us either run away or fight. In our modern world, however, we rarely have to resort to one of those actions, and yet we still feel discomfort at the physical sensation of anxiety. Our minds try to manage that discomfort by leaving, convincing ourselves that it isn't so scary, or making ourselves look bigger to feel more powerful.

Unfortunately, the effect of this fear on our brain generally means that we get defensive and assume the worst. We quickly begin weaving a story that tries to make sense of the situation, and we often end up overreacting or creating a great deal of stress for ourselves. We also tend to be a lot less empathetic and don't consider the context of the situation. Instead of seeing someone who is hurting, we see someone who is angry.

Discussion Questions:

- Have students talk about a time when they were caught off guard and they felt anxious. What was the outcome of that situation? Did it cause a great deal of stress for a prolonged period of time or cause an argument?
- Has anyone experienced anxiety that lasts long after the inciting incident is over? Has anyone ever found themselves lying awake, reliving a discussion or scenario that went sideways, and worrying about the long-term effects of it?
- What kind of self-talk do students engage in when they are anxious? What about after the stimulus is gone?

Activity: Relaxation Strategies (see Appendix A)

Meditation: Change as a Constant

Sit in a comfortable position, and close your eyes. Breathe deeply in and out a few times to settle in and clear your mind.

Picture yourself lying on your back in the ocean. You are close enough to the shore to see it, and if you stand up, your feet will touch the sandy ocean floor. The water is warm and fairly calm, but as you lie there, you can feel yourself rising up and down with the movement of the waves.

Life is a lot like the ocean; there are ups and downs, and it can be rough at the edges. When you are on the shore, you can see the waves coming toward you and anticipate when they'll break, even if sometimes they are bigger than you expected. This perspective gives us a false sense of control and lets us believe that we can predict what will happen. However, when you're lying on your back, rising up and down with the gentle movement of the waves, it is harder to know where we are.

Lie there and just let your body relax with the movement of the ocean for a few moments. Know that nothing frightening will happen—you can't sink or get overtaken by a crashing wave. You are simply letting the water lift you over and over again.

When we go to the ocean, we expect there to be constant change and movement. The messages we write on the sand will be washed away, the tide will encroach and then recede. However, while these little things change, the big picture remains mostly the same. Let that be a metaphor for your life.

We often get anxious about change, about approaching new things, and we try to control them by learning enough to think that we can predict them or by denying them and pretending they aren't there. What if we saw our lives as we do the ocean? What if we acknowledged that there will be ups and downs, things will be written and erased, and through it all, we can ride the motion knowing that the big things—our values and who we are at our core—won't change unless we choose that? What would that feel like?

Rest and breathe deeply with your eyes closed for another minute as you feel the ocean moving in synch with your life. When you're ready, take a deep breath, and open your eyes.

NOTES

1. Gottlieb, Daniel. 2008. *Learning from the Heart: Lessons on Living, Loving, and Listening*. New York: Sterling Publishing Co.

2. Shapiro, Shauna. March 10, 2017. "The Power of Mindfulness: What you Practice Grows Stronger." Video retrieved from https://www.youtube.com/watch?v=IeblJdB2-Vo.

Appendix A: Activities

These activities are designed for use with the lessons indicated in the previous chapters, although there are some supplemental activities as well that can be used on their own. You may photocopy and distribute these as hard copies to students for use during class or on their own. Unless indicated, all of these worksheets/activities were developed by the author and should be cited as such. They are not to be reproduced for purposes of sale to anyone or distribution to anyone other than the students in your class.

The majority of these exercises are for students to use on their own. You may use class time to explain and introduce them, but students should feel free to take them home and think about them before completing them. Many of these tasks will feel uncomfortable or complicated in the beginning, and others will feel very personal and private. Students need not share their answers with anyone. The ultimate goal is to increase students' ability to be introspective and self-aware and ask questions that will help them integrate the material presented in class.

MINDFULNESS WORKSHEET

Lesson: Energy Follows Intention

Activity: Mind v. Body

We live in a culture that places a high value on our thoughts and our brains. We often take our bodies for granted unless there is something wrong, such as when we are in pain or hungry or tired. Our brain and our body work best as a team, but by the time we hit middle school, most of us need a little practice tuning in to what our bodies are telling us. We have all had times when we decided to do something even though our "gut" told us not to, and we have all had times when we listened to our bodies and ate an entire pint of ice cream or two orders of fries despite the voice in our head saying, "NO!"

Fill out the following table with ideas of what a typical day in your life might look like if you only lived according to your brain (in one column) or your physical impulses (in the other column).

Use a separate sheet of paper or your journal to answer the four questions and explore the ideas introduced in this lesson.

Table A.1

Brain	Body

1. Think of times in your life when you were able to blend thoughts and emotions effectively. What did it look like? Was it hard to do?
2. What happens when we do things impulsively or emotionally without checking in with our head?
3. What happens when we discount our feelings and make choices based solely on rational thought?
4. Do you feel differently about times when you used your head more than your heart? Do you think the outcomes were different? How?

Students can sometimes struggle with the answers to these questions, and that's OK. The point is to get them thinking about how often they react emotionally to situations in their life versus how often they shut down emotional responses and seek purely logical solutions. The answers will be different for everyone, and there is no right or wrong. The more we can become curious about our own motivations in certain circumstances, the more we realize we have the power to choose how to react to things in our lives and learn from those choices.

Lesson: Anger Comes from Fear

Activity: Alternative Pathways

This activity is designed for students to work in groups of three or four during class time. Ask them to identify what they think are fear-driven responses in the following scene. Auditory or kinesthetic learners may benefit from acting out the scene or seeing it acted out. Can they articulate what each of the characters was likely afraid of?

Marcus: What's up?
Jules: We need to talk.
Marcus: (laughing) Uh-oh. Should I leave and come back?
Jules: This isn't a joke. I'm serious.
Marcus: Whoa! Just trying to lighten the moment ...
(Jules looks down at the ground.)
Marcus: What the heck? Did you do something stupid?
Jules: Why would you accuse me of that? Why is that your first instinct—that I did something dumb? What if it was you that did something?
Marcus: Did I? Jeez, out with it, already! Although, it already sounds like you might be overreacting.
Jules: Maybe it's not even worth having the conversation if you're going to be like that.
(Marcus throws his hands up in the air and rolls his eyes.)
Marcus: You say it isn't a joke, but now it's you that is playing games. Tell me or don't. I'm not a mind reader!

Jules: Never mind. I can't talk to you when you're like this. You're just upsetting me.

Marcus: Whatever. You're the one who started it. Come find me when you're grown up enough to have the conversation.

Have each group talk about what the scene might have looked like if one character had admitted what they were afraid of. Does that seem like something that could actually happen?

What do students think about being able to recognize their own fears when they start to get angry? Do they think they could acknowledge their own fear at the moment? Would it change their behavior or the other person's response?

Lesson: Owning Our Stories

Activity: Dream Analysis

Our dreams can tell us a lot about what we think of ourselves and the events in our lives. There are different schools of thought with regard to determining what our dreams mean, and one of them says that we are only capable of dreaming about things from our own perspective, which makes sense. We can't exactly get inside someone else's mind, no matter how much we want to, and if we examine our dreams from that context, we may learn something about our fears and hopes and current mindset.

1. Think of a recent or very vivid dream you've had, and write down the details. Who were the characters? What did they do or say?
2. Imagine that each of the characters in your dream (animal, human, mythical creatures, etc.) represents some part of you, and try to figure out what your subconscious could have been trying to tell you. See an example below.

Sample dream analysis: I once had a dream that I was at my mother-in-law's house cutting apart team softball photos of my daughter to give to family members. About halfway through, I realized that I had been cutting the tablecloth that was beneath the photos as I cut the photos apart. Just as I had that horrible realization, the scissors stopped cutting straight and veered off to the side in my hand. No matter what I did, I couldn't get them to cut straight—they would only cut off to the left side. In this scenario, the scissors, the photos, the tablecloth, and I are all different parts of me.

- *I represented the part of me that wanted to be in control, even if it meant destroying something else (the tablecloth).*
- *The tablecloth represented the part of me that was being harmed by my controlling ideas.*

- *The scissors were the part of me that, when they recognized harm was being done, wouldn't cooperate.*
- *The photos were the part of me that need to be separated into neat, tidy piles to distribute to the people in my life—an image that I wanted to represent myself. However, as the scissors veered off to the left, they distorted that image in the name of disrupting the controlling part of me.*

Lesson: Mindfulness and Conflict

Activity: Knot Journaling

Think about a piece of rope with a knot in it. When we are in conflict with someone, we pull on one end of the rope while the other person stands at the opposite end pulling in the other direction, and the knot represents the conflict. Think about how if your goal is to undo the knot the only way to do it is to move to the middle and work together. Otherwise, you only pull the knot tighter.

Take a few minutes to journal about a conflict—it could be one you currently have with someone else, one you can feel coming soon, or one in the recent past. The knot is the central point of contention. Think about whether you can see a way to move toward the center and work with the other person to undo it. Identify what your ultimate desired outcome is, and try to imagine what the other person's goal is. Examine whether you think it's possible to undo the knot so that you are all happy or if you think it is more likely that you will have to agree to disagree and leave this piece of rope tangled up.

Lesson: The Trap of Superlatives

Activity: Superlatives Journaling

Think about a time when you were persuaded to do something by someone who said, "Everyone else is going." Did you really believe that "everyone else" was going? Did you think that all of the people you know were going to do the same thing? Chances are you didn't really believe that. However, imagine if the person trying to convince you had said, "Fifty-three percent of your friends are going." Would that have sounded ridiculous? This activity is meant to start you thinking about the way we use words to get what we want and the impact of our words in certain situations. Write down the answers to the following questions on a sheet of paper or in your journal.

1. Think about a time when you used a superlative to convince someone else of something that you really cared about. Write down who you were

talking to, what you wanted them to do (or not do), and what your exact words were as far as you remember them. (Example: One night as they were finishing dinner, a mother stood up and said to her kids, "Nobody ever offers to help me make dinner around here. It's all my responsibility all the time." She said that to shame her kids into offering their help in the future.)
2. Now write down whether what you said was 100 percent accurate. If it wasn't, think about why you chose to say it the way you did and write that down. (Example: Nope, it wasn't true at all. Occasionally, the kids do offer to help make dinner, but they hadn't for a while, and she was missing their help. She was trying to make them feel guilty.)
3. Finally, consider how you could express your feelings differently in the future without using such extreme words (that aren't likely true). (Example: The mother could say, "Man, I could really have used some help getting dinner on the table tonight. Would one of you be willing to help me tomorrow night?")
4. Think about how the other person responded to your first way of doing things versus how you imagine they might react if you said it without using superlatives. (Example: After their mother's outburst, the kids got defensive and immediately reminded her of times when they had helped with dinner. They all left the table upset with each other. Had she said it the other way, they would have understood that she wanted help rather than the kids feeling blamed for something.)

Lesson: Living Your Values

Activity: Personal Crest

Family crests and coats of arms were widely used in Europe to denote the values and regions of noble families. They were often ornate and had things ranging from animals to flags to labels and other items of significance. This activity builds on those with the idea that there are key things that are integral to the person you are that can be represented on your own personal crest.

Design it however you want to. Perhaps you create a background that has a shape that is representative of something important (i.e., if you love music, you could have your background resemble a vinyl record album, or if you have a great deal of compassion, perhaps a heart shape is more appropriate). Spend some time thinking about the kinds of activities you enjoy, the values you hold dear, and what a representative animal might be. You can use key words or phrases and embellish the design as much as possible.

COMPASSION

Lesson: Seeing Others in Pain

Activity: Struggling with Compassion

Write down your answers in a journal or notebook. If there is time in class and you want to, share some of your answers with your classmates. This can help promote understanding and discussion of times when we all struggle to be compassionate.

1. Write about a time when you found it challenging to have compassion for someone else. Maybe it was seeing a homeless person on the street who was drunk or high; maybe your little sister borrowed your favorite shirt without asking, and you were so angry that you couldn't listen to her explanation or apology; perhaps a friend of yours told others a story about you that he or she had vowed to keep a secret.
2. Write down how you felt. Were you angry? Fearful? Don't worry about explaining or justifying your emotions; just name them. It is likely that there was more than one strong emotion; write them all down.
3. Repeat this exercise for one or two other times when you found it hard to have compassion for someone else. Think about how you felt—are there patterns? Even if the situations were very different, maybe there were some similarities. Do you think that could be why you reacted without compassion?
4. Think about what it might look like if you were able to set aside those strong emotions and try to have compassion for the other person. Is there a way you could benefit personally from doing that?

Lesson: Differing Perspectives

Activity: Assigning Feelings

This exercise shows how alike we all are, despite our actions, and can help students understand the perspective of someone they have demonized. It is designed to be done as a class. Write this list of emotions on a whiteboard or large sheet of paper for everyone to see:

Angry	Sad
Shameful	Powerful
Frustrated	Rejected
Nervous	Overwhelmed
Righteous	Superior
Distraught	Fearful

Isolated	Uncertain
Powerless	Defeated
Vulnerable	Embarrassed
Persecuted	Jealous
Confused	Hopeless

Assign one color pen to "the bully" and another color to "the victim." Have the group tell you which feelings the bully might be experiencing and use the corresponding pen to put a hash mark or circle around each. Now, have them do the same with the victim, using the other color. Notice whether there is any crossover.

- Have students discuss their assumptions and impressions of what makes someone decide to bully someone else. Are there other feelings they would add to the list?
- Ask students whether it changes their perception of a "bully" to think that they are acting out of sadness or fear instead of anger.

Lesson: Name-Calling v. Owning Your Emotions

Activity: Accepting Circle and Emotional Mirror

Improv games are great for building compassion because they get kids to think creatively and collaboratively. Acting requires looking at things from a unique perspective and helps groups coalesce because they are all looking silly together. Do these as an entire class.

Accepting Circle

Students stand in a circle, and one person begins by making a small gesture, with or without an accompanying sound. The person to their left must copy that gesture and sound (if included) as closely as they can. The fun comes in when someone in the circle involuntarily moves or makes another noise. Even if it isn't their turn, the person whose turn it is next must incorporate that sound/gesture into what they are doing. Students must watch for moans or sighs or sneezes or laughter and add them in when it's their turn.

Emotional Mirror

This game is for pairs of students. Have them sit or stand facing each other. The first person assumes a particular emotion and begins talking in nonsense words. The second person must respond with nonsense words as they mirror the emotion of the first person. The first person then assumes a different emotion and begins speaking, and the second person must again mirror the emotion and respond. After two rounds, the second person gets to be the one to choose the emotion.

Lesson: Myths and Misperceptions about Bullying

Activity: What Does Bullying Look Like?

This activity can be done with the entire class or students can make notes on their own. Some of these scenarios can be difficult to discuss calmly with a large group, but it may be important to attempt it. Alternately, you can do a silent vote on which incidents constitute bullying and present the final tally to the class so that they can see where they differ from their classmates.

Read over the following incidents and decide which ones seem like "bullying" to you. Why or why not?

Next, think about whether or not you would speak up if you witnessed any of these things and what that might look like. Students can make notes in their journal or notebook if they prefer.

- A Latino student and an Asian student have an argument that escalates into screaming racial slurs and a physical altercation while other students watch.
- The opposing football team refuses to take the field against a team with a female player because "girls have no place in boys' sports."
- Students play an off-campus game they call "Beat the Jew" where one student is the "Jew" and the others are "Nazis" who chase him or her.
- A teacher discovers a "burn" page on Facebook filled with hateful, bigoted comments directed at a student who is thought to be gay.
- A group of students wearing T-shirts with letters on them which spell out the school's name post a picture on social media where they have rearranged themselves to spell out a racial slur and call it a joke.
- The school pep rally involves students pretending to be illegal immigrants while other students, armed with billy clubs, round them up. (The students being "rounded up" are symbolizing the opposing team they will play that evening.)
- An anonymous Instagram account is created that shows candid shots of girls at school taken without their permission, and the captions denigrate the girls' physical appearance, critique their outfits, and call them sluts or whores.

Lesson: What Don't You Know?

Activity: Actor's Nightmare

Have two students get up in front of the class, and give one of them a script. The student with the script begins by choosing one of the characters and reading a line. The other student has no script and no understanding of the plot, but they must respond and try to carry on in a way that makes sense. After a few minutes, choose two more students to play the game. If you want to make it more challenging, find a scene with three actors and give two of them scripts, and then have one student play along without knowing their lines.

Afterward, ask the students who performed without the script what it felt like to not have all the information they needed to play along.

Some samples of scripts can be found at www.freedrama.net.

Lesson: Self-Compassion

Activity: Self-Compassion

Self-compassion is about removing the lens of "other" and not worrying about how others see us, and it can be hard to do so when we are feeling unsure about ourselves. It is especially difficult to do when we have made a mistake or failed at something. What follows are nine steps you can go through to develop a sense of self-compassion when you've messed up, based on the work of Drs. Kristin Neff and Christopher Germer.

Have students look over the following as they think of a time when they felt particularly bad about themselves. They can write about how one or more of these messages could shift their perspective the next time they're judging themselves harshly.

1. Recognize that some tasks are just really complicated.
2. Remember that nobody is born knowing how to do everything.
3. Acknowledge that we all fail way more often than we succeed.
4. Realize that you don't control all of the circumstances that affect success or failure. Luck is sometimes a real thing.
5. Remember that your worth does NOT equal your achievements. If it did, babies wouldn't be worth much, but everyone loves babies!
6. Recognize that it is hard to have perspective in the moment. We are often overcome with emotion when things don't work out the way we wanted them to, but a week or a month later, they don't seem like such a big deal.
7. Acknowledge your feelings, and allow yourself to be disappointed in the outcome, but make sure not to project into the future—don't assume that this one mistake means that you'll never get anything right again.
8. Remember that things we tell people are often about our successes. We don't often see failures or mistakes posted on Facebook for the world to see.
9. Comparing yourself to others is impossible because what you see of other people's lives is only the tip of the iceberg.

Lesson: Alternative Forms of Wealth

Activity: Wealth Mapping

This activity can be done by individuals or in small groups or pairs. It can be helpful for students to work with others to get additional ideas for their own wealth mapping, but each student should complete their own map.

Have them work to identify their unique stores of wealth, given their life experience and family/community design. They may come up with new types of wealth as well, and you can have them share examples with the class to generate discussion. Give students creative license to create their map with hash marks or examples of specific kinds of wealth. They can also note specific individuals who have either given them that wealth or helped them develop it. Some might discover that certain areas overlap or one might be a subset of another. Categories they might include are:

- Aspirational
- Family
- Social capital
- Navigational
- Resistant
- Linguistic
- Cultural
- Community
- Artistic

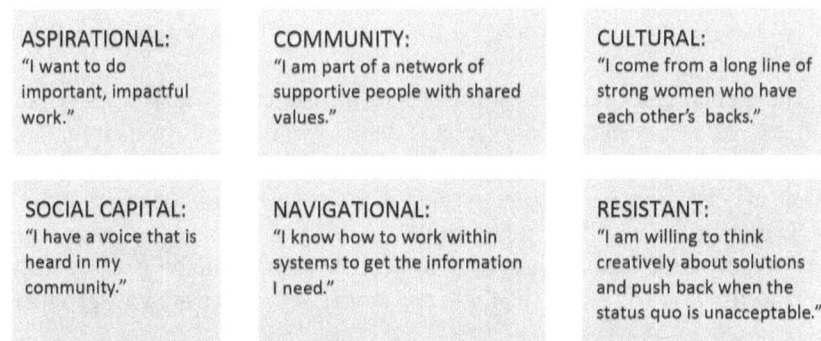

Figure A.1   Sample Wealth Map.

POSITIVE MINDSET

Lesson: Altruism

Activity: Bookend Your Day

Encourage students to create an index card or Post-it Notes with these questions on them to use at home. They can begin each day with the three morning questions and ask the evening questions during their routine before going to bed as a way to frame the day. Explanations of each of the questions are below.

Morning Questions

1. What can I expect from today?
2. What can I do to make today great?
3. What can I do for myself today?

Evening Questions

1. What made me happy today?
2. How did I help someone else today?
3. What am I looking forward to tomorrow?

Morning Questions Discussion

The first question is designed to help you wrap your head around what's happening today. Maybe you have PE and that will impact what you wear, or it makes you happy because it's your favorite class. Or perhaps you have a huge test and then a lacrosse game after school and then you have to race to the library to work on a group project that is due tomorrow, and it's going to be a crazy day. Whatever it is, this gives you the opportunity to frame your day.

The second question gives you a chance to rise to the occasion. It doesn't ask, "What would make today great?," which would imply something happening to you. It places the opportunity on your shoulders to do something to make the day great—maybe you can start your day with your favorite drink or, knowing that you'll be racing from one thing to the next, use your lunch hour to get a head start on that group project. It can be something big or small, but ideally, it is something that will cause you to feel satisfied at the end of the day.

The third question involves self-care, and it's a cool thing to get into the habit of doing for yourself every day. You deserve to be cared for, and if you don't do it, some days nobody else will. Maybe you can take a long, hot bath before bed, or you might plan to have lunch with someone who makes you feel great. Maybe you can go for a short run or swim or take fifteen minutes to sketch for fun or read a chapter of a book that doesn't have anything to do with school.

Evening Questions Discussion

The first question is solely focused on gratitude. What went well today? What surprised you or made you smile spontaneously? Look back at the day, even if it was ultimately overwhelming and exhausting, and intentionally remember a moment when you smiled.

The second question uses the knowledge that giving makes us feel connected and happy. Did you help someone with a tough math question? Hold the door for that student on crutches? Buy your little sister a coffee before school? Help your mom make the salad for dinner? It doesn't have to be big, but it's important to remember it, and pat yourself on the back for it.

The last question gives you a reason to get out of bed tomorrow. There has to be something to look forward to—even if it's your customary cup of chai tea or the fact that it's Friday. Alternatively, if you can't think of anything, create something. If tomorrow is looking like a total slog on all accounts, set up a lunch date with a good friend or plan on heading to the library to look up some of the stupidest jokes you can find and tell them to your friends.

Lesson: Deserving Joy

Activity: Finding Purpose and Meaning

Sometimes it's hard to decide what we would most like to be spending our time doing. Especially when we have absorbed messages from our parents and teachers and other outside influences telling us what we ought to do, it is difficult to hear our own voice reminding us of what we are passionate about. These five questions, adapted from a set written by author Mark Manson, can help you pinpoint some things that light you up, that put a fire in your belly. Scribble, doodle, or write your ideas in a journal or notebook. It may take a day or a week to come up with answers, and they might change over time. That's OK. The point is to start to think about the things that make you happy and figure out ways to spend more time doing them.

1. What can you stand to do even when it's hard? *The fact is that everything sucks sometimes. However, if you love horses, you'll tolerate mucking out stalls and conditioning saddles. If skateboarding is your favorite pastime, you'll practice that ollie flip a million times before you land it once. So think about it, what can you stand to do, even when it sucks?*
2. What were your favorite things to do when you were seven or eight years old? *Usually, at that age, we had more free time and fewer people telling us what we ought to do more of (practice piano, conjugate Spanish verbs—whatever). What was it that you loved most? Reading comic books? Building with Legos? Sketching or writing goofy songs? Write those things down. If you mourn the loss of them in your life, it might be time to think about ways to fit them back in.*
3. What makes you forget to eat and poop? *Have you ever been so consumed by a book or video game that you nearly peed your pants? Or have you been painting something or cooking and realized that the entire day has gone by without you eating a thing? Think about the qualities of that activity that make time pass quickly and shut the rest of the world out. Is it the challenge of the video game? The creative process of painting or cooking? The characters in a book? Whatever it is that makes you block out everything else is probably pretty important to you. Try to identify some other activities that would offer you that same intensity.*
4. What fantastic ideas do you have that you're afraid to look silly doing? *Worrying about your friends making fun of you is not a good reason NOT to do something that excites you. (Potentially causing harm to yourself or someone else IS.) Many of the best inventions came from someone taking a risk and thinking outside the box. These risk takers didn't listen to the voices (inside their heads or outside them) that said they couldn't do this or that, they weren't smart/savvy/strong enough, or that they had a crazy idea. They leaped knowing that it might fail.*
5. If you had to leave your house in the morning and not come back again until after dark no matter what, where would you go and what would you do? *This is, after all, what most people with full-time jobs do—leave home every day and not come back until dark, or some version of that. We might as well be doing something we enjoy with all of those hours. Sure, at first you might say you'd spend your time going to the movies or sitting on the beach, but how long would that interest you? What would you REALLY do? Would you go talk to strangers on the street and hear their life stories? Would you help build a neighborhood garden? Would you go to a music studio and jam? What would be awesome to do all day every day for a while?*

Lesson: Finding Joy

Activity: Gratitude Practice

Gratitude is something that gets easier the more you do it. Sometimes, when we are in the middle of a challenging time, it's hard to come up with reasons to feel good, but frankly, that's the most important time to do it.

Start by writing down things that you're grateful for in your life on a sheet of paper. You can doodle or scribble them in any way that feels good to you. Sometimes unlocking gratitude requires unlocking creativity, so don't feel as if you have to stick to writing words on lines. The first few things might seem puny—a soft pillow, a dry place to sleep, a certain friend—but as you write, you might discover that the floodgates open and you are able to think of a long list of things that you are happy to have in your life.

A quick note about gratitude—it doesn't start with "at least I'm not . . .". If you're comparing your life to someone else's or thinking about all the ways things could be worse, that's not ultimately going to make you feel good. Gratitude also isn't a balance sheet—don't weigh how many "good" things you have in your life against the number or heft of "bad" things. Gratitude should stand on its own.

When you're done with this exercise, you can tuck the paper away and look at it again. You might try to spend a few minutes every day coming up with a short list of things for which you are grateful, and if you're feeling stuck, try simplifying. Look around; you might see a computer that prompts gratitude for the ability to connect to important ideas and friends online. You might catch sight of a glass of water on the table and thank goodness for clean water to drink and bathe in, or you may see your sunglasses lying on the counter and smile at the thought of warm sunshine on your back.

Lesson: Connection

Activity: The Rule of Five

The Rule of Five states that the five people you spend the most time with have the most impact on you. There is some scientific evidence that emotions are contagious, so even if you are feeling moody, encountering a person who is acting happy and goofy can start to turn your day around.

Often, especially as teens, we can be chameleons with our friends, taking on some of their personality traits when we hang out with them for a while. Fill out the table with the names and strongest personality traits of the five people you spend the most time with, and note whether your mood or personality changes the more time you spend with them.

Table A.2

Name and Relationship	Three Strongest Qualities/Personality Traits

Now, write down a short list (five or six things) that you hope describe you and that you want to be known for. Compare your list to the things in the table and determine whether those people help you be the person you want to be.

Lesson: The Three Crowns

Activity: Goal-Setting

We all have goals. Unfortunately, sometimes those goals turn into expectations, and if things don't go the way we thought or hoped they would, we can get frustrated or disillusioned and want to give up. This activity can help you plan goals that are realistic and set yourself up to be more successful. (Although, failure is often a good thing, too, because it can teach us a lot.)

1. Identify a goal that is important to you, and write it down. (Start with something short term, like getting an A on an essay or making the varsity soccer team or getting that part-time job you want.)
2. Think about why that goal is important to you, and write that down. (What does this goal mean to you? What will it say about you to important people in your life if you accomplish it?)
3. Be honest about what it will take to achieve your goal, and write that down. (Imagine the kinds of things that might get in your way. For example, a family trip this weekend might make it hard to practice enough or read all the research. If you're a person who tends to procrastinate, be honest with yourself about that.)
4. Determine what constitutes acceptable progress, and write that down. (You may not get an A, but you might get a better grade than you did on your last paper. Can you see that as success, even if you didn't hit the mark you set? Push yourself toward the original goal, but decide if there is some other way to gauge your progress, too.)
5. Decide what you want to learn from this experience, and write that down. (The destination is important, to be certain, but so is the journey. If you don't end up achieving your goal, can you find places to do better next time or ways to access other resources that can help in the future?)

Lesson: Finding Meaning

Activity: Living a Life of Intent

Answer the following questions to learn a little bit more about yourself and the way you see the world. This exercise can be a powerful reminder of ways that we can interact with others in a positive, intentional way instead of reverting to our regular habits of reacting to the world as it comes to us.

1. What is the best thing you think has ever happened to you? What did you learn from it?
2. What is the worst thing that has ever happened to you? How long did it last? How long did you think it was going to last? What did you learn from that experience?
3. If you could go back in time three years and visit your younger self, what advice would you give you?
4. What are you most grateful for?
5. What do you think your life will be like in the future? What do you want it to be like?
6. Of all the things you are learning, which ones do you think will be the most helpful when you are an adult?
7. If you were going to be famous, what would you want to be famous for? Why?
8. What is one thing you are really good at or know really well that you can teach others?

SELF-WORTH

Lesson: Comparison as a Form of Self-Judgment

Activity: What Makes You Unique?

It's pretty common for us, especially as teenagers, to be nervous or worried about how others see us. This happens most often when we are faced with a new situation—starting a new job or school, or some alteration of our regular routine. When that nervousness gets the best of us, we can convince ourselves that we are going to have a horrible day, that everything is going to go wrong (and maybe some things already have—it could be a bad hair day or you spilled something on your sweatshirt with no time to change), and it sets us up for a rough day. This short exercise can give you a way to reset your expectations and attitude before you walk into a new situation.

Close your eyes and take a few deep breaths. When you are relaxed, make a mental list of some things that make you unique and special. Are you generous? Funny? Loving? Clever? Artistic? Musical? When you have a short list in your head, choose your favorite thing, and hold it in your mind. Picture the word itself or find a picture that represents it for you. Does it have a color or a shape? Is it cartoonish or realistic? Once you have a solid picture of it in your head, think of a few ways you show this trait in your life. Take a minute to pat yourself on the back for showing this part of yourself to the world. When you're ready, open your eyes.

This is a great way to remind yourself of the unique qualities that make you the person you are, and the more you keep those thoughts present in your mind, the more likely you are to exhibit them throughout the day. If you want to, write those unique qualities down on a slip of paper, and then tuck it into your backpack or pocket. It's a powerful reminder of who you really are, no matter what anyone else thinks.

Lesson: Shame

Activity: Self-Compassion Inventory

This activity is designed to help you be more self-aware of feelings of low self-worth and determine strategies to combat them. Take a few minutes to write your answers to the following questions in a journal or notebook. There is no need to share your responses with anyone unless you want to. In some cases, it can feel really good to hear what other people think about these things because it proves you're not alone.

1. What triggers self-criticism for you? *Do you get upset when you don't perform as well in school or sports as you want to? Are you hard on yourself about your physical appearance or the quality or quantity of friendships you have? Think about the times when you start to call yourself names or get down on yourself, and see whether there are any patterns. Are there certain people in your life who trigger your own self-criticism?*
2. What happens when you start talking negatively to yourself? *Can you recognize it as negative self-talk, or do you do it so automatically that you begin to believe it? Does this kind of talk help motivate you to try harder or be something you think other people want you to be? Are you able to talk back to it sometimes? If so, when? Are there some times when it is harder than others?*
3. When things get hard in your family or group of friends, who do you take care of first? Second? Where do you rank overall? *We are often told (especially girls and women) that helping others before helping ourselves is something to be proud of, that it is selfless and honorable. However, the truth is, if we don't care for ourselves, we don't have anything left to care for others when they need us. When people see you taking care of your own needs, they get the message that you think you are important, and they will treat you better. How often do you ignore your own needs*

in order to help someone else? Can you think about small ways to change that? Can you practice making yourself a priority?
4. How do you talk to yourself when you are feeling upset? *Most of us fall into a few categories here; we either judge ourselves ("Seriously? Why is this bugging me? It's no big deal."), we avoid the feeling by getting busy or pushing it aside, or we give ourselves a break ("Everyone struggles sometimes. It's OK if I feel bad right now; I'm only human."). What do you say to yourself when you get upset? Does it depend on what you're upset about? How can you work to be more accepting of the way you feel no matter what is going on?*

Lesson: Fitting In

Activity: Authentic People and Values

1. Think about some individuals you admire most—people who are strong, courageous, and/or committed to their lives and values. They don't all have to be people you know in real life. Make a list—it can be two or twenty people.
2. Determine whether there are similarities among the people you've listed. There might be a professional athlete and a family member, a CEO and a bus driver, but because you see these individuals as role models, there are probably particular qualities that they all share. (Generally, the people we revere are those who are very clear on what is important to them and what isn't. Does that feel true for you?)
3. Make a list of your values. Remember that our values can change over time, and that's OK. It is also OK to value different things; there are no right or wrong answers. If you are having trouble coming up with a list of values, try using these questions to prompt you:

- What are your favorite things to do?
- Who are your favorite people? Why?
- What is your default emotion?
- What things make you terribly angry?
- What things make you terribly sad?
- What things make you incredibly happy?
- What could you do without for the rest of your life?
- What are you most afraid of losing in your life?

Examples of common values: family, service, food, nature, spirituality, health, justice, survival, physical pleasure, art, rest, companionship, peace, competition, community, communication, survival, solving problems, travel, humor, honesty, winning, laughter, music, and so on.

Lesson: Platonic Ideals

Activity: Stories I Tell Myself

We all have stories we tell ourselves that play over and over again in our brains—generally, we do so without even realizing it. Often, those stories are adaptive; they help us do things more quickly, like shortcuts. However, sometimes they can become a crutch and, in the worst cases, they can become ways that we trash ourselves. Do you have friends who say, "I suck at math/history/science"? Is there someone in your family who is known as the goofball or the lazy one?

Very often, it is those narratives that keep us from being able to do some of the things we really want to do. Other times, they excuse us from even trying something challenging or exploring new ideas. The fact is, we are all capable of doing much more than we let ourselves think we are, but we have to recognize the stories that are holding us back before we can decide whether we want to change them.

Look over the sample answers from someone who has always believed that she "sucks at money" to get an idea of how you might answer the questions. You'll find a blank worksheet to complete on the next page.

Stories I Tell Myself
About: Money

1. That I'm no good at managing it.
2. It is too complicated for me to understand.
3. I'm too old to figure it out now

What is my reaction to this story line?

Ultimately, it means I'm off the hook for even trying. I get to let my husband do it all, worry about it on his own, and I don't have to be responsible for teaching my kids how to manage money as they grow up. And if I overspend, I can always shrug my shoulders and point to the first three answers and say I warned everyone.

How does this make me feel about myself?

Stupid. Lazy. A little bit guilty.

Does it feel bad enough to warrant a change?

Yes.

How can I change these stories to make my life better?

1. Ask someone who is good with money to teach me.
2. Admit that I'm scared to screw it all up.
3. Remind myself that I'm smart and I can learn anything if I really want to.

4. Find examples of things I found really challenging before that I am pretty good at now.
5. Acknowledge that it will take practice, and I will make mistakes, but the reward is that I get to feel good about myself, and maybe I won't end up destitute.

What Are the Stories I Tell Myself?

About:

1.
2.
3.

What is my reaction to this story line?

How does this make me feel about myself?

Does it feel bad enough to warrant a change?

Yes/No

How can I change these stories to make my life better?

Lesson: Pressure to Perform

Activity: Shame Progression

Christopher Germer is a clinical psychologist who teaches and practices mindfulness and self-compassion to help combat feelings of shame and worthlessness. He has developed a theory that feelings of shame come as we follow this progression of thoughts:

1. I don't like this feeling.
2. I wish I didn't feel like this.
3. I shouldn't feel like this.
4. I am wrong to feel like this.
5. I am a bad/stupid/worthless person.

Can you recall a situation in your life where you were filled with shame? Write down some details, and see if this progression of thoughts feels accurate to you.

The leap from #2 to #3 is critically important for determining whether we move into shame and worthlessness. Can you identify the assumptions you made in that situation that led you to the belief that you "shouldn't" have felt the way you did? Write them down.

What does shame feel like?

What does it sound like in your head?

The next time you start down the path of #1 and #2, can you think of things to do or say to yourself that might interrupt the progression?

STRESS, ANXIETY, AND FEAR

Lesson: Going It Alone

Activity: Short-Circuit the Anxiety Reaction

Most of us know what anxiety feels like: sweaty palms, racing pulse, queasy stomach. For some of us, that reaction can come out of nowhere and really wind us up until we are almost paralyzed, and when you're in the middle of it, it is nearly impossible to do anything but react to the physical symptoms. This activity takes advantage of the way our brains are wired to interrupt those feelings and bring us back down to earth, and it's a valuable one to practice when you're feeling stressed.

When we are feeling anxious or stressed, it is our amygdala (the part of our brain responsible for the fight/flight/freeze reaction) that has taken over. It can feel really overwhelming, but the good news is that there are some simple ways to short-circuit the increasing nervousness we feel.

Find a small, hand-size object such as an orange or a tennis ball or a rolled-up pair of socks, and pick it up with your left hand. Toss it lightly up into the air to the right, and catch it in your right hand. Now toss it lightly back to the left, and catch it in your left hand. When you're anxious or having a panic attack, this activates the connections between the two sides of your brain and shifts the blood flow away from the emotional amygdala. Any sort of action that activates the neural pathways between the two hemispheres of the brain can help you calm down, so if you don't have a tool handy, you can hop from one foot to the other or draw a line with your left hand and then draw one with your right.

Once the physical reactions to stress have calmed down, you can more easily activate the portion of your brain that has rational thought and either deal with the stressor or simply go on with your day.

Lesson: Fear, Wisdom, and Equanimity

Activity: Cracking Up Your Inner Critic

We all have an inner critic; that voice that is always judging us, telling us we aren't smart enough or pretty enough or popular enough, comparing us to others and reminding us that we have to do better.

- *You're going to fail.*
- *You always screw this up.*
- *Nobody really likes you.*
- *What makes you think you're so special?*

It is really hard to listen to that all the time, and it's hard to extinguish that voice. The truth is that voice is there for a reason—to keep us safe. It is there to instill caution, but it gets worked up pretty easily, and instead of warning us that a python is hanging from a branch above our heads, it starts to worry that we'll look ridiculous or say something that will upset others. Once it gets on a roll, it can feel pretty horrible to listen to that voice because it always sees the world as a threat. The trick is to learn how to put it in its place. Here is one way to do that:

The next time that voice starts to echo in your head, play with it. Change it to pig Latin, or give it the voice of Theodore the chipmunk or someone with a horrible accent. Repeat the words in your head, and see how silly they sound. If you have a smartphone, there are some free apps you can download that will change the sound of your voice. Speak the words in your head out loud, playing them back in different ways (such as a robot, helium, mosquito, and choir settings—I dare you not to laugh out loud). The spell can be broken pretty quickly, and once it is, we can take a deep breath and recognize that it is just the chattering of a frightened little mouse instead of our true inner compass.

Keep a "voices in my head" journal, which you will use to chronicle the times when you get down on yourself. This helps you be more aware of the kinds of things you say and, often, writing these things down makes them seem less powerful. See if you can identify patterns (i.e., Does it happen most right before a big test or game? When you are feeling rested, does it happen less?).

Lesson: How We Freak Ourselves Out

Activity: Dealing with Social Anxiety

Imagine a time when you were really frightened or anxious about something—speaking in public or trying out for the varsity sports team or displaying a piece of your artwork—and go through the following steps, writing down your answers to help solidify them in your head.

1. Awareness—Try to remember what the voice inside your head was telling you when you were most afraid. Don't try to defend yourself or talk back or judge the message; just hear the words as though you

were eavesdropping on a conversation at another table. Learning just to observe and not react is a great way to disarm anxiety. Writing those thoughts down can take away some of their power.
2. Flexibility—Ask what you expect of yourself in certain social situations. Do you have to be dressed a certain way, talk a certain way, and/or hang out with a particular group of people? Think about whether you could offer yourself some more options, and think about what that might look like. What might the reactions be? How would you handle them, especially if they resulted in negative self-talk?
3. Choice—Practice choosing other options. Take baby steps if you have to, but gradually widen your scope so that you don't have to adhere to only one narrow set of guidelines for how to be. See what that feels like.
4. Keep going—Fake it 'til you feel it. Even if you don't have the confidence to keep trying it, if you know your goal is to have more freedom to be who you are, then the more you do it, the easier it will become.
5. Talk about it—If you have close, trusted friends or family members, talk about what you're doing. Get support, and let them know that you're doing this really hard thing but that you're committed to being more comfortable with yourself. Remember that lots of times, you'll inspire someone else to try it or give them enough courage to do it too.

Lesson: The Power of Story

Activity: Calming Physical Reactions to Anxiety

Because our brains and bodies are so connected, when we get stressed or anxious, we have physical reactions to those thoughts. Taking a few minutes to pay attention to what is happening in our bodies has the effect of stopping the train of thought that is making us uncomfortable, and it allows us to take control of the physical symptoms and reverse them.

Recall a time when you were feeling overwhelmed by fear or stress and go through the following steps, writing comments on a sheet of paper or in a journal.

1. Name the feeling (e.g., "I am afraid/nervous/scared/stressed").
2. Notice where the feeling affects you physically (Heart racing? Palms sweaty? Stomach in knots?).
3. Breathe in deeply for a count of five, hold it for a count of one, and exhale for a count of five. Repeat this four times and then notice if the physical symptoms have changed at all.
4. Identify exactly what you are worried about (e.g., "I am afraid that I will look like an idiot and everyone will make fun of me").

5. Draw a picture of your fear or stress. What color is it? How big is it? What shape does it have?
6. Put the picture on the other side of the room from you and look at it. Move it around. Turn it upside down. Does it feel different now that the fear is outside of you?
7. Do something with that picture. Can you fold it up and recycle it? Crumple it up and shoot baskets with it? Tear it into little pieces? Turn it into something else by adding to it?
8. Take a minute to reflect on your physical reaction now. How do you feel?

Lesson: Rewiring the Brain to Chill

Activity: Relaxation Strategies

Anxiety can become a habit that is difficult to break. Once we set a pattern of second-guessing ourselves, we often tend to stress out about future events as well, and that starts a vicious cycle where we are constantly looking out for potentially disastrous situations. If you ever find yourself lying awake or beginning to panic about something going on in your head, try one of these relaxation strategies:

1. "Fishing Net" brain—Try to see your brain as a big fishing net, the kind that they use to haul enormous fish into a charter boat. Is it tightly woven so that even tiny fish and small bits of seaweed get caught in the net? This is your brain when it is extremely anxious. Do your best to relax the net and allow the strands to pull farther apart so that the little things slip through. As you relax the net, let go of tension in your face and neck as well. Those small things that slip through decrease the weight on you as well.
2. Find a scrap of paper and a pen or pencil, and write down exactly what you're thinking about. Determine if it is something in the past or something in the future. Then remember that you are here in the present, right now, and that is the only place you can be. Let your past or future worry drop. You can't change the past, and you can't predict the future.
3. Look at the cartoon drawing of the dog barking at the door. Create thought bubbles for each of the people at the door. Realize that even though they are both seeing the same thing, they are having very different reactions to it, and remember that the stories we tell ourselves have the power to determine how we react to everything in our lives. See if you can change your perspective on the situation that is making you anxious. Can you be the person smiling at the dog?

Figure A.2 Greeting or Warning? *Source*: Created by Lauren O'Driscoll.

ADDITIONAL ACTIVITIES

General Class Discussion or Journaling Activity

Pick a quote associated with a particular lesson, and encourage students to discuss their perspective on it or journal their thoughts and interpretations of it.

Blindfolded Movement

Students can do this in class or try it at home. It is safest to do this with at least one other person around who isn't blindfolded. If they do it at home, it is best to choose an activity that they are very familiar with, such as brushing their teeth before bed or folding their laundry and putting it away. If they do it in school, make sure it is something they do nearly every day without even thinking, such as making their way from the classroom door to their desk or getting their jacket and backpack out of an already open locker and putting them on.

Have the student put on a blindfold and make sure they can't see anything. Ask them to perform the identified task and make sure that all other folks in the area are as quiet as possible. Ask the student to notice how much more slowly and deliberately they are moving. Ask them to notice how much more they pay attention to other things such as their hands and feet and the sounds around them.

Not knowing what to do or what to expect forces us to pay attention. As soon as we think we know where we are, we stop paying attention. Ask the student (and the bystanders) if they can recall a time when they walked to school or the corner store and by the time they got there they couldn't actually remember the walk. Our minds are so powerful and used to analyzing everything and jumping ahead that we don't always pay attention to what we are doing unless we are confused or a little bit afraid.

Remembering this activity can prompt students to be mindful of other routine activities they perform. When we practice mindfulness in small, everyday ways, we are exercising the portion of our brain that makes conscious choices and remains curious about the world around us. Those things come in handy when we are faced with conflict or uncertainty.

Walking Meditation

Have students line up single file outside. This can take place on school/community center property or in a natural setting nearby. The rules of the walk are as follows:

- No speaking
- No touching another person
- No music

The goal is to have students pay attention to sounds, smells, and sights as they walk. They are encouraged to breathe deeply, listen to the sound of their feet on different surfaces and the cars or birds or other noises around them, touch things along the path such as plants or fences or walls, and really experience the different sensations that they don't normally attend to.

The leader should walk at a slower pace than normal, and the space between students in line ought to allow for comfortable personal space. The walk can last as few as five minutes or as many as twenty (this feels like a long time for most students when there is no talking or music) followed by a discussion to share observations. Some may have felt uncomfortable; others may have noticed things they never did before.

Alternative Forms of Communication

This activity is to be done in class. Divide students into pairs, and have them sit facing each other. One student is to tell the other one a short story—it can be true or made up, funny or shocking, or even fairly mundane—while the other student listens, and does their best not to react at all. The listening student should be told (separately from their partner so they can't hear the instructions) not to move or talk or even adopt any facial expressions. They should keep their face and body entirely neutral throughout the story as much as possible. When everyone is finished, have the class discuss what that may have felt like to both the speaker and the listener.

- How hard was it to not react?
- How hard was it to not get a reaction?
- What does that tell us about all of the ways we communicate with each other using nonverbal tactics?
- Does this have implications for texting or email or phone calls or other not-in-person interactions?

Listening as a Skill

Ask students to raise their hand to indicate whether they've ever had an adult tell them to "listen."

Now ask them to keep their hand raised if they've ever had an adult teach them how to "listen."

Ask students to raise their hand to indicate whether they've ever had an adult tell them to "pay attention."

Follow up by asking them to keep their hands raised if they have ever been taught how to "pay attention."

Ask students to pair off, and designate one person as the speaker and the other one as the listener. The speaker tells a short story, and the listener does their best to pay attention and listen. When the story is over, have the speaking student write down whether they felt as though the listener was truly listening to them and paying attention and why. What cues did they use to determine this? Have the listening student write down whether they were truly listening and paying attention and list the things they did to indicate that to the speaker.

Ask students to share their responses and see if they can decide what it means to really listen and pay attention to someone else. Does it vary from person to person?

The Disagreement Vacation

This activity is designed to show us how habitual it is for us to disagree with others or feel the need to make our perspective known. Students should pick one person in their life that they are close to—a best friend or sibling or parent—and attempt to go one entire day without disagreeing (aloud) with anything that person says or does. It's important that they don't let the other person know that they are doing this, however.

Have them keep notes, noticing how often their instinct is to rebut that person's statement or explain why their idea is better. Can they hear the voice in their head saying, "That's not true," and they have to keep from saying it? How often does it happen in any given day? What is their body's response to this exercise? Throughout the day, does it get easier or harder to do? Are they storing up arguments to use the next day when they can "finally" disagree again, or are they learning that it doesn't really matter? Ask them to report on the quality of their interactions with the other person when they aren't disagreeing with them.

It's true that one hallmark of a good relationship is the ability to hold different viewpoints and maintain a strong connection, but many of our interactions with other people are more about making ourselves heard than they are about learning and exploring new ideas. Hopefully, this exercise will help students learn to discern when it is important to share our perspective and when it doesn't matter.

Self-Critique Worksheet

The next flow chart/worksheet was designed to help adolescents think more deeply about the qualities they have that make them unhappy. Often, many of the assumptions we make about ourselves are things that we take for granted, but when we can look at them more critically, we realize that they fall into one of two categories: either we have no control over them, or we think we can't change them (or that it is too hard to change them). Having students work their way through this exercise can give them some insight into how they face the troubling narratives they've created about themselves and offer them either acceptance or the power to make a difference in their own lives.

Understanding Your Temperament

Have you ever noticed that you have some friends who rarely get upset and others who get mad super easy? You probably know some people who are really adventurous and those who prefer routine and caution. Some people you hang out with are more intense, while some are pretty mellow and chill, goofy folks and more serious folks, introverts and extroverts.

While we can all exhibit some of these personality traits from time to time depending on circumstances, we all tend to have an underlying temperament or default setting to who we are. Maybe people who knew you as a child told

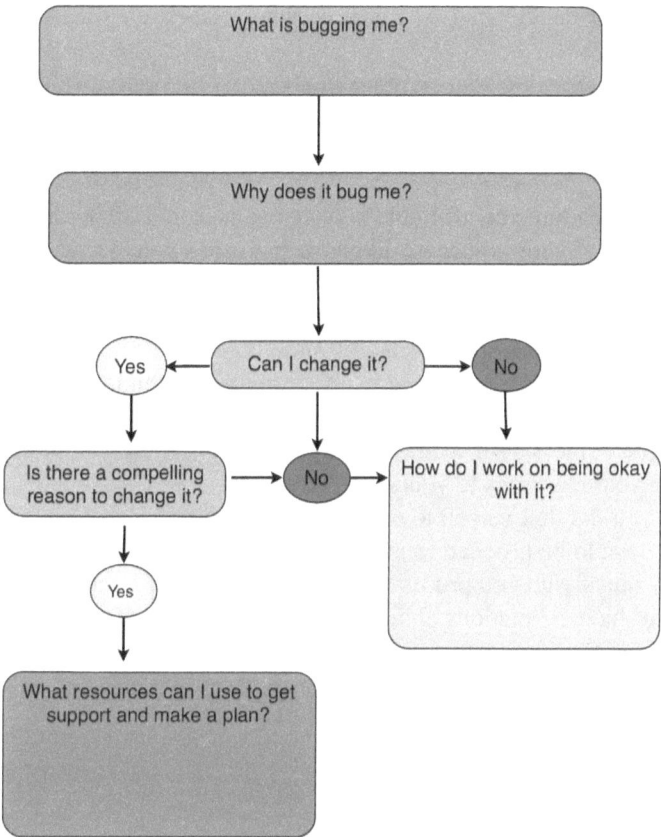

Figure A.3 Self-Critique Worksheet.

stories about how inquisitive you were or how you'd try anything to get a laugh. Can you identify your individual nature or temperament?

Knowing how you naturally react to the world around you can be a great help as you advocate for yourself in different situations. For example, if you know that you tend to be easily distracted, you can ask for a quiet area to work on a project. If you tend to be physically cautious, you can opt out of a group activity that might feel really overwhelming to you—like riding dirt bikes on the sand dunes. The more you understand your own personal preferences, the more you can ask for what you need. Answer the following questions to explore your temperament:

1. Are you more likely to want to know the rules of a game ahead of time, or would you rather learn as you go?

2. Are you a daydreamer or someone who focuses on what's in front of you?
3. Are you someone who is more likely to work alone, or do you prefer working in groups?
4. Do you often consider the big picture, or are you more concerned with details?
5. Do you feel more comfortable making big decisions after consulting your emotions, or are you more likely to put aside your feelings and try to decide with pure logic?
6. Are you more driven by fear or anticipation?
7. Would you rather spend a day off quietly reading or engaging in something creative or in the middle of a group of friends doing something together?
8. Do you express your feelings easily and often, or are you more likely to keep your emotions to yourself?
9. Are you the first person to offer an answer to someone's question, or do you have to be prodded to give your perspective?
10. How quickly do you process information? Are you someone who continues to have revelations about something you learned (or someone said) for days afterward or do you move on pretty quickly and let things go—especially if you didn't understand it right away?

Appendix B: Skill Reference Guide to Lessons

Table B.1 is designed to help educators choose individual lessons based on the particular things they want students to work on. CASEL (Collaborative for Academic, Social, and Emotional Learning) has identified five key areas of social-emotional health, although they are all interconnected and build on each other.

Table B.1

Lesson	Self-Awareness	Self-Management	Social Awareness	Relationship Skills	Responsible Decision-Making
Mindfulness: Energy Follows Intention	√	√			√
Mindfulness: Anger Comes from Fear	√	√	√	√	√
Mindfulness: Owning Our Stories	√	√			
Mindfulness: Mindfulness and Conflict	√	√	√	√	√
Mindfulness: The Trap of Superlatives	√	√	√	√	
Mindfulness: Living Your Values	√	√	√	√	√
Compassion: Seeing Others in Pain	√		√	√	√
Compassion: Differing Perspectives			√	√	

Table B.1 (Continued)

Lesson	Self-Awareness	Self-Management	Social Awareness	Relationship Skills	Responsible Decision-Making
Compassion: Name-Calling v. Owning Your Emotions	√	√	√	√	√
Compassion: Myths and Misperceptions about Bullying	√		√	√	√
Compassion: What Don't You Know?	√		√	√	√
Compassion: Self-Compassion	√	√		√	√
Compassion: Alternative Forms of Wealth	√		√	√	
Positive Mindset: Altruism	√	√		√	
Positive Mindset: Deserving Joy	√	√			√
Positive Mindset: Finding Joy	√	√			
Positive Mindset: Connection		√	√	√	
Positive Mindset: The Three Crowns	√	√		√	√
Positive Mindset: Finding Meaning	√	√	√	√	
Self-Worth: Comparison as a Form of Self-Judgment	√	√	√		
Self-Worth: Shame	√	√		√	√
Self-Worth: Fitting In	√		√	√	√
Self-Worth: Platonic Ideals	√		√	√	
Self-Worth: Pressure to Perform	√	√	√	√	√
Stress, Anxiety, and Fear: Going It Alone	√	√			√
Stress, Anxiety, and Fear: Fear, Wisdom, and Equanimity	√	√			√

(Continued)

Table B.1 (Continued)

Lesson	Self-Awareness	Self-Management	Social Awareness	Relationship Skills	Responsible Decision-Making
Stress, Anxiety, and Fear: How We Freak Ourselves Out	√	√	√	√	
Stress, Anxiety, and Fear: The Power of Story	√	√			√
Stress, Anxiety, and Fear: Rewiring the Brain to Chill	√	√			√

About the Author

Kari O'Driscoll holds bachelor's degrees in biology and philosophy from Pacific University in Oregon. She has worked in physical and mental health settings as well as schools and writes about social justice issues, parenting, mental health, and medical ethics. Her work has appeared in online journals and print anthologies, and she is active in her community, volunteering with the food bank and being on the board of a local nonprofit. She is the mother of two strong, clever, compassionate daughters and is on a mission to let teenagers everywhere know that, despite the bad rap they often get, they are amazing.

www.ingramcontent.com/pod-product-compliance
Lightning Source LLC
Chambersburg PA
CBHW030146240426
43672CB00005B/288